THE ULTIMATE HOMEMADE *Dog Food* COOKBOOK

Vet-Approved, Affordable, and Nutritious Recipes for a Healthy and Happy Dog

Petra Rice

Do you want your gift?

Scan the QR code below and get your bonus

TABLE OF CONTENTS

INTRODUCTION

Chapter 1

Welcome to the World of DIY Dog Food

As pet owners, we frequently seek ways to provide our canine companions with the best possible care, as diet plays a crucial role in their overall health and happiness. *Dog Food Cookbook* digs into the exciting and newly emerging world of DIY dog food, enlightening you, loving dog owners, with the benefits of choosing homemade meals over commercial eatables as well as starter recipes you can try out for your furry companion.

DIY FOOD VS. PROCESSED FOOD

In recent years, the conversation around pet nutrition has gained significant attention, especially regarding the food we provide our much-loved canine companions. Among the most discussed topics is the choice between DIY (do-it-yourself) dog food and commercially processed options. We need to understand the distinctions between these two types of dog foods to get out of this dilemma. After this, we can start to make the necessary wise decisions about the food we give our beloved dogs and how it affects their health and well-being.

Processed Dog Food: A Closer Look

Processed dog food, kibble, and different types of canned food are essential in many households. Dog owners can use them conveniently, they have a long shelf life, and they have other options to suit different life stages and kinds of breeds. However, the ingredients and processes behind this food production can be complicated and sometimes need to be clarified.

Most processed dog foods are articulated to meet the basic nutritional needs of the dogs, but there are certain preservatives, additives, and fillers added to the mix to increase their shelf life and make them more appealing. However, the number of ingredients might be of lower quality, and sometimes, the dog food's nutritional balance might not match our dog's needs. The high heat and pressure used during the manufacturing of these items might lower the food quality by degrading the beneficial nutrients in this food.

DIY Dog Food: A Fresh Perspective

On the other hand, DIY dog food is a more adapted approach to pet nutrition. When you prepare dog food at home, you have control over the quality of the ingredients and food that your beloved dogs consume. Using this method of nutrition, you can keep artificial preservatives and harmful additives far away from their diet. By avoiding these harmful ingredients primarily found in commercial products, you can make healthy food for your dog while keeping his needs in mind. In dog food preparation, you can modify different food recipes by considering their health concerns, like sensitivities and allergies. You can use fresh ingredients, high-quality food, and healthy substitutes during dog food preparation at home. That results in better health outcomes for your dog.

DIFFERENCE BETWEEN DIY FOODS AND PROCESSED FOOD

When considering dog food, DIY food and processed food can differ in terms of quality, nutrition, and overall impact on your dog's health. The primary differences between DIY food and processed food are as follows.

1. Ingredients and Quality

DIY Food:

Ingredients: It usually consists of whole, fresh foods like grains, meat, vegetables, and supplements. You can have complete control over the quality and source of ingredients.

Quality: Homemade Food is generally fresh and contains high-quality ingredients. It can help you avoid fillers, preservatives, and artificial additives commonly found in processed food.

Processed Food:

Ingredients: Processed food is usually prepared from a mixture of grains, meat, vegetables, and other processed ingredients, which might include artificial fillers, additives, and preservatives.

Quality: The quality of processed food varies broadly. Premium brands usually use high-quality ingredients, while low-quality brands may use less desirable fillers and components.

2. Nutritional Control

DIY Food:

Customization: When making homemade food or homemade dog food, you can customize the food according to the specific needs of the dogs, such as allergies or different health conditions.

Nutritional Balance: Careful knowledge and planning help you achieve balanced nutrition. It is really important to ensure that all the essential nutrients are present in the diet in appropriate amounts.

Processed Food:

Convenience: Processed Food is mainly formulated to meet the specific nutritional standards set by the AAFCO (Association of American Feed Control Officials).

Consistency: It usually provides a balanced diet with certain nutrient levels. It helps us to identify that the food is reputable and meets specific quality standards.

3. Health Impact

DIY Food:

Benefits: If cooked correctly, your dog will have better digestion and fewer allergies. The fresh ingredients can help you sustain their health and vitality.

Risks: One risk associated with DIY food is nutritional imbalance. In this case, careful preparation is needed to avoid contamination and ensure complete nutrition.

Processed Food:

Benefits: Processed Food is convenient and usually formulated to give your dog balanced nutrition, including minerals and vitamins.

Risks: If a brand is using low-quality ingredients and additives, it can damage your dog's health and badly impact your dog's lifespan.

4. Cost and Convenience

DIY Food:

Cost: Homemade Food can be more expensive if you choose high-quality ingredients. It is also pretty time-consuming to prepare, as it requires knowledge of dog nutrition.

Convenience: In order to prepare DIY food, you need enough preparation time and planning. Meals are less quick to serve compared to processed food.

Processed Food:

Cost: The cost of processed food might vary. Premium options can be costly, but some budget-friendly choices are also present.

Convenience: If you are a busy pet owner, this could be the ideal choice. It is easy to store and ready to serve, and it requires no preparation at all.

5. Safety and Regulation

DIY Food:

Safety: Homemade Food should be handled carefully to avoid contamination. This will help ensure that the food is ready and safe to eat with properly balanced nutrients. A pet nutritionist should be consulted.

Regulation: It is less regulated than commercial food. The owner is responsible for safety and balance.

Processed Food:

Safety: It is subject to regulatory standards and a process to control quality. Commercial food must meet nutritional and safety standards.

Regulation: Government agencies mainly regulate it to ensure compliance with nutritional requirements and safety standards.

6. Transparency

DIY Food:

Transparency: When you prepare food for your dog at home, you know what is happening. You can select and monitor each ingredient of your dog food.

Processed Food:

Transparency: The list of ingredients added to your dog food might be available, but the source and quality of your ingredients may not always be clear. However, some brands are more transparent than others.

BENEFITS OF DIY FOOD FOR YOUR DOG

DIY dog food has various advantages for your pet's well-being and health. Let's have a closer look into the key benefits of this DIY food:

Improved Nutritional Control

The basic advantage of using DIY dog food is its ability to control the nutritional content of your beloved dog's diet. This method of food preparation assures you that you are providing a balanced diet to your dog. You can maintain a balance between fats, minerals, vitamins, and carbohydrates that aligns with your dog's nutritional needs. This nutritional control over food can help with health concerns more efficiently than the other commercial groups.

Enhanced Ingredient Quality

In this method of food preparation, you get to choose fresh vegetables, whole grains, lean meat, and any other fresh nutrients. This can reduce the artificial additives and low-grade fillers that are usually present in processed food. If you choose ingredients that are rich in nutrients, it can boost your dog's energy level by improving their food intake.

Customized Meal Plans

Every dog's dietary needs vary as each dog is unique in certain factors, such as activity level, breed, age, and health status. This method of DIY dog food permits you to customize meal plans to meet your dog's individual needs. For example, if your dog needs a customized plan for weight management or any health-related issue, you can customize recipes to meet their individual needs more efficiently.

Freshness and Taste

Fresh food in DIY food gives it a pleasant and natural flavor. This is why DIY food appeals more to dogs than commercial food. Many dog owners have seen that dogs become more excited, energetic, and enthusiastic about food during mealtime when they are served fresh and homemade food. This helps dog owners feel more satisfied as their dogs enjoy their mealtime. It also helps them make healthy bonds with their dogs.

Reduced Risk of Contaminants

This method of preparation will reduce the risk of contaminants like toxins and harmful bacteria that are mostly linked with mess-produced pet foods. Proper food handling and hygiene are really important. Its overall risk can be lower with DIY food as compared to processed options.

Enhanced Digestive Health

The high-quality dog food can be prepared with homemade natural ingredients. These natural ingredients are more digestible for your dog than commercial food products. The fresh ingredients of this food have a relatively better balance of nutrients and fibers. This balanced nutrition helps your dog to digest quickly and reduces the chances of risky healthy behaviors such as diarrhea and constipation. Apart from this, avoiding preservatives and artificial additives will reduce the risk of gastrointestinal upsets caused by synthetic ingredients.

Weight Management

The other benefit associated with DIY dog food preparation is that you have full control over the portion sizes and ingredient choices. This control over the food portion helps you manage your dog's weight. By making a balanced meal with healthy fats, carbohydrates, and proteins, you can manage your dog's ideal weight. This personalized approach can help prevent obesity and associated health problems, confirming that your dog maintains a healthy weight.

Stronger Immune System

Preparing high-quality dog food at home helps strengthen your dog's immune system. The more high-quality and fresh food your dog uses to eat, the stronger the immune system will be. The reason behind this is that fresh food is rich in vitamins and antioxidants, and the minerals present in food support overall immune function and can help fight oxidative stress. Ingredients like fruits and vegetables, often richer in homemade diets, provide necessary nutrients that strengthen your dog's ability to fight off infections and illnesses far better and stronger.

Increased Bonding Time

Preparing food for your dog can be a bonding activity that will strengthen your relationship with your buddy. The whole process of choosing your dog's favorite food, picking healthy and fresh ingredients for that food to cook, and also serving that favorite meal to your dog allows you to spend quality time with your dog and nurture a deeper connection. This practical approach can help you better understand your dog's liking and dietary needs.

Adaptability to Special Dietary Needs

Another advantage of DIY food is that it allows easy adaptation to your dog's special nutritional needs. For certain health conditions, like kidney disease and diabetes, you can adjust the ingredients accordingly. This level of flexibility guarantees that you can provide a food that supports your dog's health and well-being in a way that commercial foods cannot offer.

Overall, boarding on the journey of DIY dog food offers an exciting opportunity to enhance your dog's food and health. By understanding the differences between DIY and processed food, and recognizing the benefits of homemade meals, you can make a well-informed decision that best suits your dog's specific needs and preferences. With perseverance and care, DIY dog food can be a pleasant way to show your love and commitment to your furry friend's well-being and help you both stay active and healthy so you can have a good time together.

Part 1

Canine Nutrition Fundamentals

Chapter 2

NUTRITIONAL NEEDS OF DOGS

Understanding your dog's nutritional needs is vital for providing a diet that supports their general health and well-being. Like humans, dogs also need a balance of macronutrients and micronutrients to flourish. While going through this chapter, you will understand the specific nutritional components essential for dogs, including carbohydrates, proteins, fats, vitamins, and minerals. Once we have broken down each of these elements, you'll gain a complete understanding of what and how much it will take to keep your canine companion healthy and happy.

MACRONUTRIENTS

Macronutrients are the primary nutrients required to offer energy and support growth and bodily functions. For dogs, these macronutrients are proteins, fats, and carbohydrates. Each macronutrient plays a discrete role in maintaining the healthy well-being of your beloved dogs.

Proteins

Proteins are the central macronutrient in the dog's diet and the building blocks of the body. They are essential for growth and muscle development and also help repair tissues. Proteins are made up of amino acids, some of which are essential amino acids, which dogs cannot manufacture and must obtain through their food intake. This is why they are necessary for dog food.

Essential Amino Acids

Amino acids are the smallest units of protein. Dogs cannot prepare essential amino acids, which must be obtained from their diet. The key essential amino acids are arginine, histidine, isoleucine, leucine, lysine, methionine, phenylalanine, threonine, tryptophan, and valine. Each plays a unique role in bodily functions and growth.

Key Functions:

- **Muscle Maintenance:** Proteins provide amino acids for muscle growth and repair.
- **Enzyme Production:** Proteins create enzymes that help in biochemical reactions.
- **Immune Function:** Proteins help strengthen the immune system by producing antibodies and other components.

Protein Sources

Animal Proteins: The animal sources of high-quality protein are lamb, beef, chicken, fish, and turkey. Animal proteins are complete sources of protein as they contain all essential sources needed by dogs.

Plant Proteins: Lentils, peas, and soy are the sources of plant proteins. They are generally less complete compared to animal protein. Certain plant proteins need to be combined to get all the essential amino acids.

Protein Requirements

Puppies require higher protein levels to support rapid growth and development. Recommended levels range from 22% to 32% of the total diet.

Adult Dogs require moderate protein levels to maintain muscle mass and overall health. Typically, protein accounts for 18-25% of the total diet.

For **Senior Dogs,** protein levels may need to be adjusted depending on health conditions, generally around 20-25% of the total diet.

Carbohydrates

Carbohydrates are an essential source of energy for dogs. After their breakdown, they get converted into glucose, which helps cellular functions and activities. While not as critical as fats and proteins, carbohydrates can still be essential to a dog's diet.

Key Functions of Carbohydrates

Growth and Development: Carbohydrates are essential for providing the energy required for the growth and development of muscles, tissues, and organs in dogs. While proteins are responsible for building these structures, carbohydrates fuel the body's processes, especially during the growth phases of puppies and for maintaining body function in adult dogs.

Supporting Metabolic Functions: Carbohydrates are important for efficient metabolic processes. They help ensure that fats and proteins are used effectively in the body by providing a readily accessible energy source, which allows proteins to focus on tissue repair and growth rather than being burned for energy.

Maintaining Energy Balance: Carbohydrates play a vital role in maintaining energy balance, which supports overall bodily functions and physical activity levels, making them a critical component of a dog's diet.

Types of Carbohydrates

Simple Carbohydrates: Simple carbohydrates consist of sugars such as fructose and glucose. They provide energy but can lead to spikes in blood sugar if consumed in excess.

Complex Carbohydrates: Complex carbohydrates consist of fibers and starches in grains like oats, rice, and barley and vegetables like peas and sweet potatoes. They help maintain energy and support digestive health.

Sources: Good sources of carbohydrates for dogs include vegetables (carrots, sweet potatoes), fruits (blueberries, apples), and whole grains (oatmeal and brown rice). It's essential to pick complex carbohydrates that provide continuous energy and improve your dog's digestive health.

Carbohydrate Requirements

Puppies benefit from higher carbohydrates levels to fulfill their growing needs. Carbohydrates account for almost 30- 50 % of the total diet.

Adult Dogs: Adult dogs need a moderate amount of carbohydrates to sustain energy balance. Carbohydrates are usually 30 to 50% of the total diet.

Senior Dogs benefit from slightly reduced carbohydrate levels to prevent obesity and weight gain.

Fats

Fats are a dense energy source and vital for various body functions. They also help absorb fat-soluble vitamins, improving the health of dogs' skin and coat.

Types of Fats

Saturated Fats are usually found in animal products. They provide energy, but an excessive amount might lead to serious health consequences, such as heart disease and obesity.

Unsaturated Fats are found in fish and plant oils. These include monounsaturated fats like olive oil and polyunsaturated fats like fish or flax seeds oil. The unsaturated fats are beneficial for the overall well-being of the dogs.

Essential Fatty Acids include Omega-3 (e.g., DHA and EPA from fish oil) and Omega-6 (e.g., linoleic acid from vegetable oils). These fatty acids are vital for proper growth, development, and inflammation control.

Key Functions:

Energy Storage: Fats offer a concentrated energy source and are stored in the body for later use.

Cell Structure: Fats are necessary for the structure of the cell membrane and thus, help support cell functions.

Nutrient Absorption: Fats help absorb vitamins A, D, E, and K, also known as the fat-soluble vitamins.

Sources:

The healthy fat sources for dogs are plant oils (olive, flaxseed, animal fats) and fish oils. Omega-3 and omega-6 fatty acids can be supplemented as well as found in foods like a healthy coconut.

Fat Requirements

Puppies: To support growth and energy needs, puppies need a higher fat level. The recommended level of fats is 8 to 20% of the total diet.

Adult Dogs: Adult dogs need moderate fat, around 5 to 15 % of the total diet. The amount depends on the dog's health and activity level.

Senior Dogs: Senior dogs need lower fats to avoid weight gain associated with health problems.

MICRONUTRIENTS

While required in smaller amounts than macronutrients, micronutrients are crucial for a dog's development and overall health. These include vitamins and minerals that play vital roles in numerous physiological processes. Understanding the significance of each micronutrient, their sources, and how to ensure adequate intake through diet is essential for maintaining optimal health in dogs.

Vitamins

Vitamins are organic compounds crucial for your dogs' immune function, metabolism, and overall health. Different vitamins play a unique role in maintaining the health of your dogs. Vitamins are organic compounds required in trace amounts for various metabolic processes. They can be classified into water-soluble and fat-soluble vitamins.

Water-soluble Vitamins

Vitamin B Complex

B1 (Thiamine): It is essential for nerve function and carbohydrate metabolism. The deficiency of this vitamin might lead to weight loss, loss of appetite, and nervous system issues. The sources of this vitamin include liver and whole grains.

B2 (Riboflavin): It is essential for producing energy and skin health. Its deficiency might cause skin issues, poor growth, and eye problems. It is found in the liver, eggs, and dairy products.

B3 (Niacin): This vitamin is essential for metabolic processes and for maintaining healthy nerves and skin. A deficiency might lead to digestive problems and skin issues. Fish, poultry, and meat are good sources of this vitamin.

B5 (Pantothenic Acid): It is involved in energy production and hormone synthesis. Deficiency is rare but can lead to digestive problems and fatigue. It is found in grains, vegetables, and meats.

B6 (Pyridoxine): It is key for immune function and protein metabolism. Its deficiency can cause seizures, behavioral changes, and anemia. It is found in poultry, fish, and meat.

B7 (Biotin): It is essential for hair growth, skin health, and energy metabolism. Its deficiency might lead to hair loss and skin disorders. Its sources include liver and egg yolk.

B9 (Folate): It is necessary for DNA synthesis and cell division. Its deficiency can cause anemia and growth issues. It is found in spinach, liver, and legumes.

B12 (Cobalamin): It is essential for the formation of blood cell formation and neurological function. Its deficiency might lead to anemia and neurological problems. Its sources include fish, meat, and dairy products.

Vitamin C

It acts as an antioxidant and supports immune function. While dogs can synthesize vitamin C, supplements can help improve immune health, particularly in ill or stressed dogs. Sources include vegetables and fruits.

Fat-Soluble Vitamins

Vitamin A

Essential for vision, skin health, and immune function. Deficiency can lead to vision problems, skin issues, and immune dysfunction. Found in liver, fish oil, and carrots.

Vitamin D

Necessary for calcium and phosphorus metabolism, crucial for bone health. Deficiency can cause bone deformities and muscle weakness. It is found in fish liver oils, among other foods.

Vitamin E

It is an antioxidant and supports immune function and skin health. Deficiency can lead to skin problems and immune issues. Sources include vegetable oils and nuts.

Vitamin K

Essential for blood clotting and bone health. Deficiency can cause bleeding disorders and bone issues. Found in leafy greens and liver.

Vitamin B

It helps in the formation of red blood cells. Vitamin B also helps in energy metabolism.

The sources of this type of Vitamin are meat, whole grains, and eggs.

Requirement of Vitamins: The need for vitamins varies; most commercial dog foods are fortified to meet these requirements. While preparing DIY foods, owners must ensure meal plans that cover all the vitamin bases.

Minerals

Minerals, as inorganic elements, play an essential role in maintaining the body's functions, such as nerve function, fluid balance, and bone health.

Requirement of Minerals: Balance is key. Too much or too little of certain minerals can cause health issues. A typical dog's diet should include a balanced calcium and phosphorus ratio (generally around 1.2:1).

Major Minerals

Calcium

Vital for bone and teeth formation, nerve function, and muscle contraction. Deficiency can lead to bone deformities and osteoporosis. It is found in dairy products, bone meal, and green leafy vegetables.

Phosphorus

It works with calcium to build bones and teeth and is involved in energy metabolism. Deficiency can lead to poor bone health and appetite loss. Sources include meat, fish, and grains.

Potassium

Regulates fluid balance, nerve function, and muscle contraction. Deficiency can cause muscle weakness and heart issues. It is found in meat, fruits, and vegetables.

Sodium

Maintains fluid balance and supports nerve function. Deficiency is rare but can cause dehydration and electrolyte imbalances. It is found in salt and animal proteins.

Magnesium

It is important for muscle function, nerve transmission, and bone health. Deficiency can lead to muscle cramps and behavioral changes. It is found in meat, grains, and green vegetables.

Trace Minerals

Iron

It is essential for red blood cell production and oxygen transport. Its deficiency might lead to fatigue and anemia. Its sources include red meat, liver, and fortified cereals.

Zinc

It is essential for immune function, wound healing, and skin health. A deficiency can cause hair loss, skin issues, and a poor immune response. It is found in whole grains, fish, and meat.

Copper

Copper is important for enzyme function, iron metabolism, and connective tissue health. A deficiency might lead to skeletal abnormalities and anemia. Copper is found in shellfish, liver, and nuts.

Manganese

Its function is to support metabolism, antioxidant function, and bone health. A deficiency can lead to growth problems and metabolic issues. The sources include nuts, leafy greens, and grains.

Iodine

It is essential for thyroid functioning and hormone production. Its deficiency might lead to thyroid disorders and growth problems. It is mainly found in iodized seafood and salt.

Selenium

It acts as an antioxidant to support immune function. Its deficiency can cause muscle weakness and immune dysfunction. It is found in grains, meats, and nuts.

SIGNS OF DEFICIENCY AND TOXICITY

Deficiency Symptoms

- **Vitamin A**: Poor vision, skin issues, and immune dysfunction.
- **Vitamin D**: Bone deformities, muscle weakness, and dental issues.
- **Vitamin E**: Skin problems, immune issues, and reproductive difficulties.
- **Vitamin K**: Excessive bleeding and difficulty clotting.
- **Minerals**: Symptoms vary by mineral but can include issues like anemia (iron), skin problems (zinc), and bone issues (calcium).

Toxicity Symptoms

Vitamin Overdose: Excessive intake of fat-soluble vitamins can lead to toxicity. Symptoms vary and might include diarrhea, vomiting, and organ damage.

Mineral Overdose: Excessive use of minerals such as phosphorous or calcium can cause serious health issues like bone abnormalities and kidney damage.

Managing Imbalances

Monitoring: Regular Veterinary checkups can help monitor micronutrient levels and detect any early imbalance.

Dietary Adjustments: You can modify your dog's diet to correct deficiencies or excesses depending on the veterinary's advice.

LIFE STAGE NUTRITIONAL REQUIREMENTS

Puppies

Nutritional Needs: At this stage, puppies need a high fat and protein content to support rapid growth and development. A balanced diet with sufficient phosphorous and calcium is necessary for healthy bone development.

Feeding Schedule: They need proper feeding frequently, almost 3 to 4 times a day, with a smaller portion than an adult dog.

Adult Dogs

Nutritional Needs: They need to maintain health and weight with a balanced level of fat, protein, and carbohydrates. Monitor their body conditions regularly to adjust their essential diet as required.

Feeding Schedule: Usually, they need food twice a day, with snacking in between.

Senior Dogs

Nutritional Needs: Protein levels must be adjusted to support aging joints and kidneys. Food with higher fiber helps with digestion, and low fat helps with obesity.

Feeding Schedule: Depending on the health conditions, more frequent and smaller meals may be required.

Pregnant and Lactating Females

Nutritional Needs: Pregnant and lactating females need high calories, fat, and protein to support milk production and puppy growth. Essential fatty acid supplements and additional calcium might be beneficial.

Feeding Schedule: They need frequent feeding with meals multiple times a day.

Working Dogs

Nutritional Needs: High maintenance dogs that are employed in the workforce eat food with higher calories to support physical activity. Additional fat and protein might be necessary to maintain performance and endurance.

Feeding Schedule: Their meal portions and frequency can be adjusted based on the activity level.

SPECIAL DIETARY NEEDS

Allergies and Sensitivities

Nutritional Needs: Identify and eliminate substances that cause allergies. A diet with limited ingredients or a protein source might be necessary.

Common Allergens: Chicken, Wheat, Beef, and Dairy.

Obesity

Nutritional Needs: To promote satiety and weight management, a reduced-calorie diet with high fiber helps with digestion. Controlled portions and regular exercise are important.

Feeding Schedule: Need smaller and more frequent meals.

Diabetes

Nutritional Needs: For diabetic dogs, a low-fat, high-fiber diet is necessary to help regulate blood sugar levels. Persistent feeding schedules and controlled carbohydrate intake are also super important.

Feeding Schedule: Portion sizes and meal timing should be consistent to maintain insulin levels.

Kidney Disease

Nutritional Needs: To decrease the workload of the kidneys, they need food with reduced phosphorous and protein. Omega-3 fatty acids and high-quality proteins might be really beneficial.

Feeding Schedule: They need smaller and more frequent meals.

Gastrointestinal Issues

Nutritional Needs: If the dog has gastrointestinal issues, they need quickly digestible diets with high fiber and low fat. Low-residue diets with novel proteins might be recommended.

Feeding Schedule: They need more frequent and smaller meals to lessen gastrointestinal stress.

NUTRITIONAL BALANCE

When you ensure your dog receives all the essential nutrients correctly and in the right amount, it is known as nutritional balance. Every dog owner aims to provide a balanced diet for their dog's well-being. This helps prevent deficiencies and excessiveness and supports overall health and long life.

Commercial Dog Food

Complete and Balanced: High-quality commercial dog foods are prepared to meet the nutritional standards established by organizations like the AAFCO. They are appropriate and designed to provide balanced nutrition.

Label Reading: While choosing the right food, understand the ingredient lists and guaranteed analysis.

Homemade Diets

Nutritional Balance: Making homemade dog food requires proper planning to ensure that all essential nutrients are included accurately. Consulting with a veterinary nutritionist is advisable.

Supplementation: You need additional minerals and vitamins to achieve a balanced diet.

Combination Feeding

Purpose: Combining commercial food with homemade meals can provide variety and additional nutrients. Balance is vital to ensure both types of food complement each other.

BALANCING NUTRIENTS

Macronutrients

Macros in a balanced diet means it should contain appropriate levels of carbohydrates, fats, and proteins. The ideal ratio of these nutrients varies with the dog's age, health status, and activity level. A generally balanced diet for average-sized dogs is as follows:

Proteins: 20-30% of the diet.

Carbohydrates: 30-50% of the diet.

Fats: 10-20% of the diet.

Micronutrients

Along with fats, carbohydrates, and protein, enough minerals and vitamins are also necessary. A pinpointed, accurate measure of micronutrients is not needed unless your dog is on a special diet advised by the vet. A balanced diet will offer a spectrum of essential vitamins and minerals, which can be attained by integrating a variety of nutrient-dense ingredients.

Monitoring and Adjusting

Monitor your dog's health, including weight, age, overall vitality, and weight, and adjust each nutrient in your dog's diet accordingly. Consultation with a pet nutritionist or veterinarian before starting any regimen, including DIY home food, is a must as they can provide recommendations on ensuring your dog's diet maintains a balance by considering its specific needs.

Before making any changes, pay attention to the quality and quantity of the nutrients in your dog's current food and introduce new changes slowly. The result will be simple: a healthy, happy, and active life.

Chapter 3

Food Safety Guidelines

The safety of our dogs is our priority. For this, we need to understand food safety, which involves determining which food is safe or toxic for dogs. This chapter delves into comprehensive food safety guidelines for dogs. After reading it, you will understand everything from purchasing and handling to preparation and storage.

UNDERSTANDING FOOD SAFETY FOR DOGS

Food Safety is based on certain practices and procedures that prevent certain foodborne illnesses, spoilage, and contamination. Dogs, like humans, are also susceptible to diseases caused by certain pathogens, such as viruses, bacteria, and parasites. Adhering to food safety guidelines helps to protect them from these risks.

Importance of Food Safety

Health Protection: Appropriate food safety practices help prevent gastrointestinal illnesses, food poisoning, and long-term health issues.

Quality Maintenance: Ensures the nutritional quality of dog food remains intact.

Prevention of Cross-Contamination: It reduces the risk of transferring harmful microorganisms from food to other surfaces or foods.

Common Pathogens and Contaminants

- **Bacteria**: Salmonella, E. coli, Campylobacter.

- **Viruses**: Canine parvovirus (though not typically transmitted through food, proper hygiene can prevent secondary infections).
- **Parasites**: Giardia, Toxoplasma.
- **Toxins**: Mycotoxins (from moldy food), chemical contaminants.

PURCHASING DOG FOOD SAFELY (COMMERCIAL)

Selecting Commercial Dog Food:

Reputable Brands: When selecting commercial dog food, always choose a brand with a history of safety and quality. Look for those that adhere to standards set by organizations like AAFCO (Association of American Feed Control Officials).

Ingredient List: Always choose high-quality ingredients and avoid foods with artificial additives, excessive fillers, or any unknown component.

Expiration Date: Always check the expiration date on the packing list to make sure you are using fresh food for your dog.

Buying from Reliable Sources

Pet Stores: Always try to purchase food from well-known pet stores with good reputations for food safety.

Veterinary Clinics: You can get the food from any vet clinic as they also offer high-quality, specialized dog food.

Online Retailers: You can order from reliable stores with transparent product information and customer reviews.

Inspecting Packaging

Integrity: Ensure the packing is intact, and there should be no damage or tampering.

Storage Conditions: Ensure the food was appropriately stored (e.g., dry and cool) before purchase.

HANDLING DOG FOOD

Hygiene Practices

Hand Washing: Wash your hands before managing the dog food.

Clean Surfaces: Maintain hygiene during the food preparation. Use clean surfaces and utensils while preparing and serving dog food.

Separate Utensils: Use separate utensils to handle dog food to avoid cross-contamination with human food.

PREPARING DOG FOOD (DIY)

Cooked Food: Use thoroughly cooked food so harmful bacteria and parasites will be removed from the cooked food.

Avoid Seasonings: Do not use spices, salt, or any other seasoning that will harm dogs.

Safe Cooking Methods: Prefer boiling, baking, or steaming methods rather than frying.

Risk of Contamination: Raw diets are at greater risk of bacterial contamination. Manage raw food carefully and stick to hygiene practices.

Safe Thawing: To safely thaw frozen raw food, place it in the refrigerator or a sealed container in cold water. Don't thaw food at room temperature.

Cleaning: Clean your hands, utensils, and surfaces thoroughly after managing the raw food.

STORING DOG FOOD

Proper Storage Techniques

Dry Food: Store dry food in an airtight container to prevent pests and moisture from entering. Keep the food in a dry and cool place away from sunlight.

Canned Food: Once the canned food is opened, refrigerate any unused portion in an airtight container so you can use it within a few days.

Raw Food: If the dog food is not used immediately, store it in the freezer. Make sure it is well-wrapped to avoid freezer burn.

MONITORING FOOD FRESHNESS

Check for Spoilage: To check dog food, see signs of spoilage such as mold, smell, or changes in texture at any time.

Observe Your Dog: Monitor your dog for any signs of unusual behavior after eating or if there are any signs of illness. That will indicate food spoilage.

MANAGING FOOD LEFTOVERS

Disposal: Discard any uneaten food left out for more than a few hours to prevent bacterial growth.

Safe Reheating: While reheating the dog food, ensure it is heated thoroughly to kill potential pathogens.

FEEDING PRACTICES

Portion Control

Feeding Guidelines: Follow the feeding recommendations according to your dog's size, age, activity level, and health condition.

Measure Portions: Use a scale or a measuring cup to provide accurate portions and avoid underfeeding or overfeeding.

Regular Feeding Schedule

Consistency: Create a regular feeding schedule to sustain digestive health and prevent obesity.

Avoid Free-Feeding: Unless the veterinarian advises otherwise, don't leave food out all day. It will lead to overeating and then weight gain.

Monitoring Your Dog's Health

Behavior Changes: Monitor your dog's behavior changes. Changes in appetite, energy levels, and stool consistency indicate dietary issues.

Veterinary Checkups: Have a regular veterinary checkup, as it will help monitor your dog's overall health and adjust its diet.

DEALING WITH FOOD RECALLS (COMMERCIAL)

Staying Informed

Subscription Services: Subscribe to pet food recall notifications from organizations like the FDA or pet food manufacturers.

Veterinary Alerts: Your veterinarian may provide updates on food recalls and safety alerts.

Response to Recalls

Immediate Action: If your dog's food is recalled, stop feeding it immediately. For returns or refunds, follow the manufacturer's instructions.

Health Monitoring: Monitor your dog for any symptoms of illness and consult your vet if any health issues arise.

HANDLING SPECIAL DIETARY NEEDS

Allergies and Sensitivities

If your dog has any food allergies, identify the allergens and remove them from your dog's food instantly. The allergens that are most commonly identified are chicken, beef, dairy, and grains.

Work with a veterinarian to develop an appropriate diet plan for dogs with food allergies or sensitivities.

Medical Conditions

Dogs with any medical condition, such as kidney disease, diabetes, or gastrointestinal issues, might need specialized diet plans provided by the vet. Consult your veterinarian for guidance on managing these conditions through diet.

Weight Management

Balanced Diet: If your dog is overweight or underweight, adjust the portion size and calorie intake in its diet.

Regular Monitoring: Monitor your dog's weight on a regular basis, and based on their weight, adjust their diet and exercise routine accordingly.

TRAVELING AND FOOD SAFETY

Packing Dog Food

Portion Control:

Pre-measure the food while traveling with your dog to avoid overfeeding and maintain consistency.

Storage Solutions: Use airtight containers or resealable bags to keep food fresh during travel.

Safe Food Handling

Food Storage: Place the food in a dry and cool place. Also, don't place it in extreme temperatures.

Hygiene: Sustain good hygiene practices by cleaning bowls, utensils, and surfaces after each use.

Adapting to New Environments

Gradual Transitions: When adding new food during travel or when there is a change in routine, do so gradually to avoid any digestive upset.

Emergency Supplies: Carry a small supply of your dog's regular food in case of unexpected delays or plan changes.

EDUCATING OTHERS

Family and Friends

Informed Feeding: Teach family members and friends about safe feeding practices and the importance of not sharing human food with dogs.

Clear Instructions: Provide instructions on handling and feeding your dog if you are away.

Dog Sitters and Caregivers

Detailed Instructions: Provide dog sitters or caregivers with detailed feeding and food handling instructions.

Emergency Contacts: Leave contact information for your veterinarian in case of any dietary or health concerns.

SAFE AND TOXIC FOODS FOR DOGS

Food safety is essential to avoid accidental poisoning and ensure dogs' well-being. Many human foods can be valuable to dogs, while others could be fatal. Let's have a detailed look at safe and toxic dog foods.

Safe Foods for Dogs

Certain foods can be healthy for your dog if provided moderately. These foods can also provide nutrients and variety.

Lean Meats

Lean meats like beef, turkey, and chicken are outstanding protein sources. Just make sure to remove any skin, excess fat, or bones, as these can cause digestive issues or choking hazards. Try to cook meats completely to avoid the risk of bacterial infections.

Vegetables

Many vegetables, such as green beans, sweet potatoes, carrots, etc., are advantageous for dogs. These vegetables are high in fiber and vitamins. They can help with digestion and maintain a healthy weight. You can provide these vegetables in raw or cooked food but don't add oils or seasoning.

Fruits

Fruits can be tasty treats for dogs. Strawberries, apples, bananas, and blueberries are good sources of antioxidants and vitamins. The only fruits to be avoided are avocados and cherries, as they have high sugar content or pits.

Plain Yogurt

Plain yogurt can be a good source of probiotics and calcium. It also helps with digestion and promotes healthy gut flora. However, be careful when using flavored yogurt containing artificial additives and sugars.

Rice and Oatmeal

Oatmeal and plain cooked rice are accessible on the stomach and help soothe digestive system issues. They are a source of carbohydrates and could be mixed with vegetables and lean meats for a balanced meal.

Toxic Foods for Dogs

Several foods can harm dogs and should never be fed to them. As a dog owner, understanding these kinds of food can prevent serious health issues or even fatalities.

Chocolate and Caffeine

Chocolates rich in the theobromine and caffeine are deadly to dogs. Small amounts can cause serious diarrhea, seizures, vomiting, and rapid breathing. Dark chocolate and baking chocolate could be particularly dangerous for dogs.

Grapes and Raisins

Grapes and raisins can be toxic to dogs, and they can lead to kidney failure. The exact toxin is not known, but even small quantities can lead to serious health consequences, such as vomiting, loss of appetite, and lethargy.

Onions and Garlic

Chives, garlic, onion, and leeks can lead to gastrointestinal upset. They can also damage the red blood cells, leading to anemia. Symptoms of toxicity include diarrhea, lethargy, and vomiting.

Avocado

The persin which is fungicidal toxin in avocados can also be toxic to dogs, eventually leading to diarrhea and vomiting. The pit, skin, and fruits should all be avoided.

Alcohol

One of the extreme poison to dogs is alcohol, which leads to severe symptoms such as diarrhea, breathing difficulty, coma, and even vomiting. Keep alcoholic beverages out of your dogs' reach at all times.

Xylitol

Xylitol, a sugar substitute found in sugar-free gum and candies, can cause a rapid release of insulin in dogs, leading to hypoglycemia (low blood sugar). Symptoms include loss of coordination, seizures, and lethargy.

Cooked Bones

Raw bones are better for your dogs as they are safe to eat. On the other hand, cooked bones can cause choking, splintering, or even tears in the digestive tract. Always avoid giving cooked bones to your dogs and try to give them raw bones, as they are easy for them to chew, swallow, and digest.

MEAL PREPARATION AND STORAGE

The following meal preparation and storage guidelines can prevent foodborne illnesses and maintain the freshness of homemade food for your dog.

Meal Preparation

Use Fresh Ingredients:

Always try to use high-quality and fresh ingredients when preparing your dog's meals. Using outdated or spoiled ingredients can lead to foodborne illnesses and damage your dogs' health. Always check the expiration dates of the ingredients before using them for your dog's meal preparation.

Cook Thoroughly

Before giving meat to your dog, cook it thoroughly so that harmful bacteria such as Salmonella and E. coli in the meat are killed completely. Raw or undercooked meat can pose health risks to your beloved dog. Try to use a meat thermometer to make sure that the meat has been reached to safe internal temperatures.

Avoid Harmful Additives

During meal preparation, don't use salts, oil, or any seasoning that is dangerous for your dog. Stick to dog-safe ingredients to ensure that meals are nutritious and free from harmful substances.

Portion Control

While measuring portions, keep the dog's size, age, and activity level in mind. Overfeeding and underfeeding can lead to weight issues and nutritional imbalances. If you are confused about this, make an appointment with the veterinarian to find out the appropriate portion sizes.

Handle Food Safely

Always try to maintain proper hygiene during meal preparation. First, thoroughly wash your hands, surfaces, and utensils to avoid cross-contamination. Also, make a routine of using a separate cutting board for raw meats and ingredients.

Food Storage

Refrigeration:

After preparing the dog meal:

- Store it in the refrigerator to avoid bacterial growth.
- If you have stored it in the fridge, try to feed this dog food within 3-5 days.
- Use an airtight container to maintain food freshness and prevent odor from affecting other foods.

Freezing:

If you want to store the dog food for longer, try making and freezing portions. This helps preserve the food and makes it convenient to serve it. First, divide the food into meal-sized portions and use freezer-safe containers or bags. Always use labels with dates to track how long the food has been frozen.

Thawing:

Always thaw frozen dog food in the refrigerator instead of at room temperature to avoid bacterial growth. Let the food thaw gradually and make sure it is fully defrosted before serving. Please don't use a microwave to thaw food because it can cause potential hot spots and uneven heating.

Avoid Leaving Food Out:

Try to avoid leaving dog food at room temperature for a longer period, as this might lead to bacterial contamination. To prevent spoilage, always use food in adequate portions and discard any uneaten food after 1-2 hours.

Monitor Storage Conditions:

It is really important to monitor storage conditions for your dog food. Dry dog food should be kept in a cool, dry place, away from direct sunlight and moisture. To maintain freshness and prevent pests from contaminating the food, try to store it in airtight containers.

Food safety is critical to providing a healthy diet to your dog. With the guidelines we discussed in this chapter, you can be vigilant and distinguish between healthy and toxic food. While we have discussed preliminary practices for proper meal preparation and storage, this aspects will be explored in detail later. Implementing these guidelines will help the dog's overall health and prevent any potential foodborne illnesses.

Chapter 4

SUPPLEMENTS AND ADDITIVES

Adding necessary supplements and additives to your dog's diet can be a good decision. This is because it will enhance their health, ensure a well-rounded nutritional profile, and will support their specific needs. In this chapter, we will go through various supplements and additives, including their benefits, sources, recommended usage, and precautions, considerations of supplements and additives for dogs, including how to select the right products and use them safely.

WHAT ARE SUPPLEMENTS AND WHEN AND HOW TO USE THEM

Supplements are dietary additions to food. They help your dog get necessary nutrients or provide different health benefits not entirely covered by its regular diet. These supplements are related to specific health issues, support the overall well-being of dogs, and ensure that your dog has a diet with nutritional balance.

Purpose and Benefits

Health Support: Supplements can strengthen joint health, digestive system, coat and skin condition, and more.

Medical Conditions: If you are using supplements for certain medical conditions, they can also help manage allergies, arthritis, and kidney disease.

Nutritional Gaps: If there is a nutritional gap in a dog's diet, supplements will help to fill it.

TYPES OF SUPPLEMENTS

Joint Health Supplements

Glucosamine: This supplement supports cartilage repair and joint lubrication. It is mostly used for dogs with joint issues or Arthritis.

Chondroitin: It is mostly given to dogs in combination with glucosamine. It helps to sustain cartilage structure and prevent degradation.

MSM (Methylsulfonylmethane): An anti-inflammatory supplement that may help with joint pain and swelling.

Omega-3 Fatty Acids: These are mostly found in fish oil. They can help reduce inflammation and support joint health.

Skin and Coat Supplements

Omega-6 Fatty Acids: This supplement helps promote healthy skin and a shiny coat. It is found in certain plant oils, like flaxseed oil.

Biotin improves skin health and coat quality. It can also help with flaky and dry skin.

Vitamin E: An antioxidant that supports skin health and can help manage skin conditions.

Digestive Health Supplements

Probiotics: Beneficial bacteria that help maintain a healthy gut flora and improve digestion and immune function.

Prebiotics: Non-digestible fibers that encourage the growth of beneficial bacteria in the gut.

Digestive Enzymes Help break down food and improve nutrient absorption. They are useful for dogs with digestive issues or enzyme deficiencies.

Nutritional Supplements

Multivitamins: They provide a range of necessary vitamins and minerals that may be missing from a dog's diet.

Calcium: It supports bone health, which is particularly important for growing puppies or dogs on homemade diets.

Iron is essential for blood health and beneficial for dogs with anemia or low iron levels.

Immune System Support

Vitamin C: An antioxidant that can support immune function. Dogs typically produce their Vitamin C, but supplements can be helpful in certain medical or deficiency situations.

Echinacea: This may help boost the immune system and improve infection resistance.

Behavioral and Cognitive Support

L-theanine is an amino acid that can help reduce anxiety and stress in dogs.

CBD Oil: Derived from hemp, it is used for its potential calming effects and support for pain and inflammation.

CHOOSING THE RIGHT SUPPLEMENTS

Assessing Your Dog's Needs

Health Conditions: First, find out if your dog has specific health conditions that require targeted supplements.

Diet: Consult any vet doctor to evaluate the current diet and determine if any nutritional gaps need to be addressed with supplements.

Consult Your Veterinarian: Always consult a veterinarian before starting any new supplement to ensure it's appropriate and safe for your dog.

Quality and Safety

Reputable Brands: Choose supplements from reputable manufacturers that meet quality standards and regulations.

Ingredient Transparency: Look for products with clear labeling and ingredient lists.

Third-Party Testing: Prefer supplements that have undergone third-party testing for quality and purity.

Form and Administration

Palatability: Choose a form that your dog will readily consume, whether it's a chewable, powder, liquid, or pill.

Dosage: Follow dosage recommendations from the manufacturer or your veterinarian to avoid overdosing or underdosing. These might vary according to your dog's age, size, and weight.

INTEGRATING SUPPLEMENTS INTO YOUR DOG'S DIET

Introduction and Monitoring

Gradual Introduction: Introduce new supplements slowly to monitor for any adverse reactions or allergies.

Observe Your Dog: Watch for changes in behavior, coat condition, or overall health to assess the supplement's effectiveness.

Adjustments and Follow-up

Adjust Dosage: Adjust the dosage of different supplements depending on your dog's response: Slight to no increase for a good response, stopping the supplementing if presented with unintended effects.

Regular Vet Checkups: Try to schedule regular checkups to monitor your dog's health and review their supplement regimen.

Combining Supplements

Compatibility: Before starting supplement(s), make sure that they are compatible with each other and do not interfere with any medication, medical treatment, or diet.

Balanced Approach: The primary aim is to have a balanced approach to supplementation, exercise, and combining diet and adequate supplements to support overall health.

POTENTIAL RISKS AND SIDE EFFECTS

Overdosing

Symptoms: Excessive amounts of certain minerals and vitamins can lead to health issues or toxicity.

Prevention: Take only prescribed dosages and consult with a veterinarian to avoid overdosing.

Allergic Reactions

Symptoms: Watch for signs of allergies like swelling, itching, or gastrointestinal upset.

Action: Discontinue use and consult your veterinarian if an allergic reaction occurs.

Interactions with Medications

Drug Interactions: Some supplements may interact with medications, altering their effectiveness or causing side effects.

Consult Your Vet: Discuss any supplements with your veterinarian, especially if your dog is on medication.

Quality Control Issues

Contaminants: Poor-quality supplements may contain contaminants or harmful additives.

Choose Trusted Brands: Opt for supplements from brands with stringent quality control measures and third-party testing.

REGULATIONS AND STANDARDS

Industry Regulations

AAFCO Guidelines: Pet supplements should comply with AAFCO (Association of American Feed Control Officials) guidelines for safety and labeling.

FDA Oversight: The FDA regulates dietary supplements, but its oversight is less stringent than that of pharmaceuticals. Look for products that adhere to high-quality standards.

Labeling and Claims

Clear Labeling: Ensure that supplements have clear and honest labeling, including ingredients, dosage instructions, and any potential side effects.

Avoid Overly Broad Claims: Avoid supplements that make broad or exaggerated health claims without scientific backing.

HOMEMADE SUPPLEMENTS AND ADDITIVES

Natural Additives

Herbs and Spices: Certain spices like turmeric and ginger can provide health benefits but should be used carefully and in small doses only.

Bone Broth: Homemade bone broth can be a nutritious addition to your dog's diet, providing vitamins, minerals, and joint-supportive compounds. Make sure no cooked bones make their way into the broth as they are harmful.

Safety and Preparation

Consultation: Always consult with a veterinarian before adding homemade supplements to ensure they are safe and beneficial.

Proper Preparation: Ensure that homemade supplements are prepared hygienically and with fresh ingredients to avoid contamination.

VITAMINS

Vitamin A

Function: It is necessary for vision, improving skin health, supporting cell growth, and immune functions.

Sources: sweet potatoes, carrots, liver.

When and How to Use: Vitamin A should be present in your dog's diet, but an excessive amount can be toxic. A well-balanced homemade or commercial diet usually has adequate amounts. If you find a need to add extra vitamin A, consult your vet before adding it.

Vitamin B Complex

Function: Includes B1 (Thiamine), B2 (Riboflavin), B6 (Pyridoxine), B12 (Cobalamin), and others that support metabolism, energy production, and red blood cell formation.

Sources: dairy, meats, whole grains, eggs

When and How to Use: These vitamins are found in adequate amounts in a balanced diet. However, supplements could be vital for dogs with certain health conditions and poor appetite under veterinary guidance.

Vitamin D

Function: It helps maintain phosphorous and calcium absorption, essential for bone health.

Sources: liver oils, liver, fish

When and How to Use: Vitamin D supplements should be used very wisely, as excess can lead to toxicity for your dogs. If a vet causes any kind of deficiency, it will be best to use an extra amount.

Vitamin E

Function: It acts as an antioxidant, protecting cells from damage and supporting skin health.

Sources: green leafy vegetables, vegetable oils, nuts,

When and How to Use: In most commercial foods, an adequate amount of vitamin E is present. Supplements should only be taken when your veterinary doctor diagnoses any deficiency.

Vitamin K

Function: It plays a vital role in blood clotting.

Sources: Liver, green leafy vegetables

When and How to Use: Usually, dogs get enough vitamin K from their diet. Supplements are only needed if a veterinary doctor recommends a deficiency.

MINERALS

Calcium and Phosphorus

Function: It helps in bone development and maintenance. The correct balance of these minerals is essential for bone growth.

Sources: meat, dairy products, bones

When and How to Use: These supplements are primarily used in homemade meals to ensure a proper balance in growing dogs with specific health conditions.

Zinc

Function: It helps support immune function, enzyme activity, and skin health

Sources: whole grains, meat, seafood

When and How to Use: Zinc supplements are mostly used in deficiency cases, which can manifest as skin problems or poor coat quality. A balanced diet usually provides an adequate amount of zinc.

Iron

Function: It is essential in producing red blood cells and transporting oxygen.

Sources: red meats, fortified cereals, liver

When and How to Use: Iron supplements are primarily used with dogs suffering from anemia or iron deficiency. Over-supplementation might lead to toxicity, so excessive amounts of iron should be avoided.

Magnesium

Function: It supports muscle and improves nerve function, as well as bone health.

Sources: seeds, green leafy vegetables, nuts

When and How to Use: Magnesium is generally present in sufficient amounts in a balanced diet. Supplementation is only given if a diagnosed deficiency exists.

FATTY ACIDS

Omega-3 Fatty Acids

Function: It helps reduce inflammation, supports skin and coat health, and contributes to overall cardiovascular health.

Sources: flaxseed oil, fish oil

When and How to Use: Omega-3 supplements are helpful for dogs with inflammatory conditions or skin issues. Dosage should be personalized based on the dog's size and health needs.

Omega-6 Fatty Acids

Function: It supports skin health, hair growth, and overall cellular function.

Sources: sunflower oil, evening primrose oil

When and How to Use: Omega-6 fatty acids should be balanced with Omega-3s to prevent excessive inflammation. Supplementation is typically included in well-formulated dog foods.

AMINO ACIDS

Taurine

Function: It is essential for heart function and eye health.

Sources: fish and meat

When and How to Use: Taurine supplementation is essential for dogs with specific health conditions, such as dilated cardiomyopathy. A balanced diet usually provides sufficient taurine.

Carnitine

Function: It helps with fat metabolism and supports energy production.

Sources: fish, red meat

When and How to Use: Supplementation is used in weight management cases or specific metabolic disorders. Sufficient levels are usually provided in a well-balanced diet.

RECOMMENDED INGREDIENTS WITH SUPPLEMENTS

1. Beef Liver:

- **Vitamins**: A, B-complex (B2, B6, B12)
- **Minerals**: Iron, Zinc, Phosphorus

- **Amino Acids**: Taurine, L-Carnitine

Beef liver is an incredibly nutrient-dense food, providing high amounts of essential vitamins and minerals, particularly B vitamins, iron, and zinc.

2. Salmon:

- **Vitamins**: D, B-complex (B3, B6, B12)
- **Fatty Acids**: Omega-3 (EPA and DHA)
- **Minerals**: Phosphorus

Salmon is rich in omega-3 fatty acids, essential for skin and coat health, and a great source of Vitamin D and phosphorus.

3. Chicken (Dark Meat with Skin):

- **Vitamins**: B-complex (B3, B5, B6)
- **Minerals**: Phosphorus, Zinc
- **Fatty Acids**: Omega-6 (from skin)
- **Amino Acids**: Taurine, L-Carnitine

Chicken provides quality protein, essential B vitamins, and omega-6 fatty acids, particularly in the dark meat and skin.

4. Eggs:

- **Vitamins**: A, D, E, B-complex (B12)
- **Minerals**: Phosphorus, Iron
- **Amino Acids**: Taurine, L-Carnitine

Eggs are a complete protein source, rich in several vitamins, especially B12 and Vitamin D, and provide a small amount of omega-3 fats.

5. Sardines (with bones):

- **Vitamins**: D, B-complex (B12)
- **Minerals**: Calcium, Phosphorus

- **Fatty Acids**: Omega-3 (EPA and DHA)

Sardines are packed with calcium (due to their bones), omega-3 fatty acids, and Vitamin D.

6. Spinach:

- **Vitamins**: A, C, E, K1
- **Minerals**: Iron, Magnesium, Zinc

Spinach is a great plant-based source of multiple vitamins and minerals, including Vitamin A and K1, iron, and magnesium.

7. Sweet Potatoes:

- **Vitamins**: A, B-complex (B6)
- **Minerals**: Potassium, Magnesium

Sweet potatoes are high in Vitamin A and a good source of Vitamin B6 and magnesium, making them an excellent source of energy and fiber.

8. Pumpkin Seeds:

- **Minerals**: Magnesium, Zinc
- **Fatty Acids**: Omega-6

Pumpkin seeds offer magnesium and zinc while also providing healthy fats, including omega-6.

9. Bone Broth:

- **Minerals**: Calcium, Phosphorus, Magnesium
- **Amino Acids**: Taurine, Glycine

Bone broth is an excellent source of minerals like calcium, phosphorus, and magnesium, and supports joint and gut health.

10. Flaxseed Oil:

- **Fatty Acids**: Omega-3 (ALA)

Flaxseed oil is rich in plant-based omega-3 fatty acids and can be added to balance the fatty acid profile for dogs.

WHAT ARE ADDITIVES?

Substances that are added to dog food to increase its health benefits, support specific body functions, and improve digestion are known as additives.

Probiotics

Function: Probiotics are beneficial bacteria that maintain gut health and improve digestion.

Sources: Specially formulated probiotic supplements; Yogurt (plain, unsweetened), Kefir, Buttermilk, Goat's Milk, Cottage Cheese (low-fat, unseasoned, unsalted).

When and How to Use: Probiotics can help with digestive health or recovery from gastrointestinal issues. Follow dosage recommendations based on the product and consult with a vet.

Prebiotics

Function: Prebiotics are non-digestible fibers that feed beneficial gut bacteria.

Sources: Pumpkin, Sweet Potatoes, Chicory Root, Apples (without seeds), Bananas, Asparagus, Oats, Flaxseeds, Blueberries, Barley

When and How to Use: Include prebiotics in the diet to support a healthy gut microbiome. They are frequently included in commercial dog foods and supplements.

Antioxidants

Function: Antioxidants protect cells from damage caused by free radicals and support overall health.

Sources: Vitamins C and E, selenium.

When and How to Use: Antioxidants can help with aging and chronic health conditions. They are frequently included in dog foods and supplements.

Chondroitin

Function: Their vital role is to support joint health and to remove symptoms of arthritis.

Sources: Chondroitin sulfate supplements; Beef Trachea, Chicken Feet, Bone Broth (from cartilage-containing bones), Green-Lipped Mussels.

When and How to Use: Chondroitin is used for dogs with joint issues or arthritis. The dosage depends on the dog's weight and health condition.

Natural Additives

Function: Various natural additives can boost health and flavor.

Natural Additive	Benefits	Cautions
Coconut Oil	Supports digestion and healthy skin	Use in moderation, can cause diarrhea if given in excess.
Turmeric	Anti-inflammatory and antioxidant properties	Too much can cause stomach upset, use small amounts.
Apple Cider Vinegar	Aids digestion and supports immune health	Should be used sparingly, excessive use can upset the stomach.
Chia Seeds	Rich in Omega-3 and fiber	Safe in small amounts, too many can cause digestive issues.
Flaxseed (ground)	Omega-3 fatty acids and fiber	Should be ground for proper digestion, use in moderation.
Bone Broth	Rich in collagen, chondroitin, and glucosamine	Generally safe, but avoid if high sodium is present.
Spirulina	High in protein, vitamins, and antioxidants	Safe in small amounts, but avoid if your dog has liver issues.
Kelp	Source of iodine, supports thyroid health	Excessive iodine can affect thyroid function, use with caution.
Dandelion Greens	Natural detoxifier, rich in vitamins	Safe, but ensure they are pesticide-free.
Parsley	Breath freshener and rich in vitamins A and C	Avoid curly parsley, which can be toxic in large quantities.
Pumpkin Puree	Great for digestion and a source of fiber	Safe, but don't use pumpkin pie filling (which contains sugar).

Natural Additive	Benefits	Cautions
Ginger	Soothes digestion and helps with nausea	Safe in small amounts, excessive use can cause gas or bloating.
Green-Lipped Mussel Powder	Supports joint health	Generally safe, consult vet for specific dosing.

When and How to Use: Add them in small amounts to a balanced diet. Ensure the additives are safe and appropriate for your dog's age and health.

OTHER USEFUL INGREDIENTS

Brewer's Yeast

Function: Provides B vitamins, supports skin and coat health, and can repel fleas.

Sources: Brewer's yeast supplements.

When and How to Use: Always use it in small amounts to support overall health and coat condition. Consult your vet for appropriate dosages.

Fish Oil

Function: Rich in Omega-3 fatty acids, supports skin, coat health, and reduces inflammation.

Sources: Fish oil supplements.

When and How to Use: Fish oil is used as directed to support skin health and joint inflammation. Adjust dosage based on the dog's size and health needs.

Eggshell Powder

Function: A natural source of calcium, it supports bone health.

Sources: Ground eggshells.

When and How to Use: Always use it in homemade diets to ensure adequate calcium levels. Follow recommended dosages to prevent over-supplementation. Overdosing might lead to serious health consequences for your dogs.

BALANCING NUTRITION, DOSAGES, AND PRECAUTIONS

Balancing Nutrition

Maintaining a balance between additives and supplements is necessary to avoid any excess or deficiency. Supplements should be matched, not replaced, as it should be a well-rounded diet. This all should be done to ensure that the overall nutritional diet of the dog is balanced. Take into account the specific needs of your dog, keeping in mind its size, age, and health conditions.

Here's a general balanced nutrition table for small, medium, and large dogs:

Nutrient	Small Dogs (<10 kg)	Medium Dogs (10-25 kg)	Large Dogs (>25 kg)
Calories	300-400 kcal/day	600-900 kcal/day	1,200-1,800 kcal/day
Protein (min 18-22% of diet)	15-20 g/day	40-60 g/day	80-120 g/day
Fat (min 8-15% of diet)	10-15 g/day	25-35 g/day	50-75 g/day
Carbohydrates	25-40 g/day	60-80 g/day	100-150 g/day
Fiber	2-4 g/day	4-6 g/day	6-8 g/day
Water	250-500 ml/day	500-1,000 ml/day	1,000-2,000 ml/day

The following table highlights the amount of per meal for according to your dog's size.

Dog Size	Dog Weight	Amount of Food (oz) per Meal	Meals per Day	Total Daily Amount of Food (oz)
Small	Up to 11 lbs	1.75-3.5	2-3	3.5-10.5
Medium	12-33 lbs	3.5-7	2-3	7-21
Large	34-66 lbs	7-10.5	2-3	14-31.5
Very Large	67-99 lbs	10.5-14	2-3	21-42
Giant	Over 100 lbs	14-17.5	2-3	28-52.5

Dosages

Dosage is a sensitive issue and must be done with great consideration. Here's a general dosage table for small, medium, and large dogs based on typical recommended amounts. Note that these are **general guidelines**, and you must consult a veterinarian for specific recommendations tailored to your dog's needs.

Nutrient / Additive	Small Dogs (<10 kg)	Medium Dogs (10-25 kg)	Large Dogs (>25 kg)
Vitamin A	1,000-2,000 IU/day	2,000-3,500 IU/day	3,500-5,000 IU/day
Vitamin B Complex	50-100 mg/day	100-200 mg/day	200-400 mg/day
Vitamin C	100 mg/day	200 mg/day	500 mg/day
Vitamin D	100-200 IU/day	200-400 IU/day	400-800 IU/day
Vitamin E	100 IU/day	200 IU/day	400 IU/day
Vitamin K	25-50 mcg/day	50-100 mcg/day	100-150 mcg/day
Calcium	500 mg/day	1,000 mg/day	1,500 mg/day
Phosphorus	500 mg/day	1,000 mg/day	1,500 mg/day
Zinc	10 mg/day	20 mg/day	30 mg/day
Iron	10 mg/day	20 mg/day	30 mg/day
Magnesium	50 mg/day	100 mg/day	150 mg/day
Omega-3 (Fish Oil)	100-200 mg/day	200-400 mg/day	400-800 mg/day
Omega-6	100-200 mg/day	200-400 mg/day	400-800 mg/day
Taurine	250 mg/day	500 mg/day	1,000 mg/day
L-Carnitine	50 mg/day	100 mg/day	200 mg/day
Probiotics	1-2 billion CFUs/day	2-4 billion CFUs/day	4-6 billion CFUs/day
Prebiotics	1/4 tsp/day	1/2 tsp/day	1 tsp/day

Nutrient / Additive	Small Dogs (<10 kg)	Medium Dogs (10-25 kg)	Large Dogs (>25 kg)
Antioxidants (e.g. spirulina)	250 mg/day	500 mg/day	1,000 mg/day
Chondroitin	300 mg/day	600 mg/day	900 mg/day
Natural Additives (e.g. turmeric, ginger)	1/4 tsp/day	1/2 tsp/day	1 tsp/day
Brewer's Yeast	1/4 tsp/day	1/2 tsp/day	1 tsp/day
Eggshell Powder (Calcium)	1/4 tsp/day	1/2 tsp/day	1 tsp/day
Fish Oil	100 mg/day	200 mg/day	300 mg/day

Notes:

- **Vitamins A, D, E, and K** are fat-soluble vitamins, so excess intake over time may lead to toxicity. Use caution and consult with a vet if supplementing over long periods.
- **Calcium and Phosphorus** should be given in balanced ratios to avoid issues with bone health.
- **Omega-3 and Omega-6**: Essential fatty acids should be balanced for healthy skin, coat, and inflammation reduction.
- **Taurine and L-Carnitine**: These amino acids are essential for heart health, particularly in certain breeds like boxers and retrievers.
- **Probiotics and Prebiotics**: Aid in gut health; doses are typically measured in CFUs (colony-forming units) for probiotics.
- **Brewer's Yeast**: High in B vitamins and supports skin and coat health.
- **Fish Oil**: High in omega-3 fatty acids and can help with skin, coat, and joint health.
- **Chondroitin**: Helps support joint health and can be paired with glucosamine for added benefits.

This table is only intended as a guide to give you a general idea; always tailor dosages to your dog's specific health needs by consulting your veterinarian for individualized recommendations.

Precautions

Avoid Over-Supplementation: Excessive amounts of vitamins and minerals can lead to toxicity. Stick to recommended dosages and consult with a vet.

Monitor for Reactions: Keep an eye on your dog when a new supplement is introduced. If your dog experiences any adverse reactions or changes in behavior, stop using the supplement and consult a vet.

Quality Matters: Choose high-quality supplements from reputable sources to ensure that your dog is eating safe and nutritious food.

After understanding the role of various minerals, amino acids, vitamins, fatty acids, and other additives, you can make informed choices that will support your dog's health. Additives and supplements can play a valuable role in supporting your dog's health, addressing specific medical needs, and improving its quality of life. Always work closely with your veterinarian to tailor a supplement regimen to your dog's unique needs and monitor their health regularly to ensure the best outcomes.

Part 2

Ingredients and Storage

Chapter 5

INGREDIENTS CONTAINING SUPPLEMENTS

Many common ingredients provide essential nutrients and contain beneficial supplements that support overall health. This chapter explores vital ingredients rich in supplements, detailing their nutritional benefits and how they contribute to your dog's well-being.

LEAN MEAT

Nutritional Benefits

Lean meats such as beef, turkey, and chicken are abundant in high-quality protein, necessary for maintaining muscles, repair, and growth. They are also brilliant sources of various vitamins and minerals.

Supplements Contained

Amino Acids: Lean meats offer vital amino acids such as carnitine, taurine, and carnitine, essential for heart health and energy metabolism.

B Vitamins: Meats are high in B vitamins, including B6 (pyridoxine), B12 (Cobalamin), and niacin (B3). These vitamins support metabolism, nerve function, and the production of red blood cells.

Iron: Needed for oxygen transport in the blood and overall energy levels.

Usage Tips

Preparation: Cook meats thoroughly to prevent any bacterial contamination. Remove any bones, skin, or excess fat before feeding.

Serving: Lean meats can be served as the primary protein source, or you can mix them with other ingredients to create balanced meals.

FISH

Nutritional Benefits

Fish is a nutrient-rich ingredient that provides essential fatty acids and high-quality protein. Common fish used in dog food include sardines, salmon, and mackerel.

Supplements Contained:

Omega-3 Fatty Acids: Fish is an abundant source of Omega-3 fatty acids (EPA and DHA), which are useful for skin health, reducing inflammation, and improving coat quality.

Vitamin D: Used to maintain calcium and phosphorus balance for healthy bones.

Iodine: It is essential for the proper functioning of the thyroid.

Usage Tips:

Preparation: Cook the fish thoroughly to remove contaminants. Don't use oils or seasoning.

Serving:

Include fish as a part of a balanced diet, either as a main ingredient or in moderation.

EGGS

Nutritional Benefits

Eggs are multipurpose and highly nutritious ingredients that provide ingredients that provide various essential nutrients.

Supplements Contained:

Protein: Eggs provide complete protein with all essential amino acids that are needed.

Vitamin A supports vision, skin health, and immune function.

Vitamins B: Includes B2 (riboflavin), ***B5*** (pantothenic acid), and B7 (biotin), which are essential for skin health and energy metabolism.

Choline: It helps in supporting brain health and liver function.

Calcium: Ground eggshells (1/2 teaspoon for small dogs or 1 teaspoon for larger dogs).

Usage Tips:

Preparation: Cook eggs well to reduce the risk of salmonella and improve digestibility. Then, scramble them or hard boil them.

Serving: You can serve eggs as a supplement to the meal and mix them with other ingredients.

ORGANS

Nutritional Benefits

Organ meats like heart, kidney, and liver are nutrient-rich and provide a concentrated source of minerals and vitamins.

Supplements Contained:

Vitamin A is higher in the liver, supporting vision and immune function.

Iron: Found in the liver and heart, essential for red blood cell production.

B Vitamins: High levels in organs support energy metabolism and overall health.

Coenzyme Q10: It is found in the heart and supports cardiovascular health.

Usage Tips:

Preparation: Cook organ meats to ensure they are safe and easily digestible. Don't use excessive amounts to prevent any nutrient imbalance.

Serving: Include organ meat in a varied diet; try to make it up as a small percentage of the food.

VEGETABLES

Nutritional Benefits

Vegetables are an exceptional source of fiber, minerals, and vitamins. Common vegetables are peas, carrots, and green beans.

Supplements Contained:

Vitamin A: Sweet potatoes and carrots are high in beta-carotene, which will convert to Vitamin A.

Vitamin C: It helps in supporting immune function. Mostly, it is found in broccoli and bell peppers.

Fiber: It helps with digestion and maintains a healthy weight.

Usage Tips:

Preparation: Cook the vegetables well to enhance digestibility and nutrient absorption. Don't use any seasoning.

Serving: Vegetables can be served raw or cooked, mixed into meals, or eaten as snacks.

FRUITS

Nutritional Benefits

Fruits are an abundant source of fiber, vitamins, and antioxidants. Blueberries, apples, and bananas are the fruits used in dog food.

Supplements Contained:

Vitamin C: Apples and blueberries provide antioxidants that support overall health.

Fiber: It helps with digestion and maintaining a healthy weight.

Potassium: It is found in bananas and supports muscle and nerve function.

Usage Tips:

Preparation: Remove pits and seeds from fruits before feeding. Always serve in moderation to prevent excessive sugar intake.

Serving: Fruits can be used as treats or mixed with any meal for added nutrients.

BROWN RICE AND OATS

Nutritional Benefits

Oats and brown rice are exceptional carbohydrates and fiber sources, providing sustained energy and supporting digestive health.

Supplements Contained

Vitamins B: Brown rice and oats provide B1 (thiamine), B2 (riboflavin), and B6 (pyridoxine) vitamins, which help with metabolism and energy production.

Fiber: It helps in digestion and promotes a healthy gut.

Usage Tips:

Preparation: To improve digestibility, cook the oats and rice thoroughly, without adding oil or seasoning.

Serving: To have a balanced meal, mix it with other protein and vegetable ingredients.

SWEET POTATOES AND LEGUMES

Nutritional Benefits

Legumes (such as chickpeas and lentils) and sweet potatoes are rich in nutrients and provide essential minerals and vitamins.

Supplements Contained:

Vitamin A: Sweet potatoes are high in beta-carotene that converts into Vitamin A.

Fiber: It helps with digestion and maintaining a healthy weight.

Minerals: Legumes provide minerals like potassium, iron, and magnesium.

Usage Tips:

Preparation: Cook sweet potatoes and legumes to enhance digestibility and increase nutrient absorption.

Serving: You can include it as the main serving in a balanced meal or mix it with other protein and vegetable ingredients.

FISH OIL

Nutritional Benefits

Fish oil is an intense source of Omega-3 fatty acids, which offer several health benefits.

Supplements Contained:

Omega-3 Fatty Acids: EPA and DHA in fish oil support skin health coat quality and lessen inflammation.

Vitamin D helps strengthen bone health and calcium absorption.

Usage Tips:

Dosage: Use the recommended dosage based on your dog's size and health needs. Over-dosages can lead to imbalances.

Serving: Fish oil can be added to meals or mixed into food.

The ingredients we have mentioned in this chapter will form the crux of your dog's homecooked meals: lean meats, fish, eggs, fruits, vegetables, brown rice, oats, sweet potatoes, legumes, and fish oil. Adequate preparation and serving practices will ensure that these ingredients will contribute to your dog's overall health.

Chapter 6

Essential Equipment for Dog Food Cooking

Cooking for your dog can be a healthy way to ensure they get the best nutrition. The right equipment makes the process more enjoyable and valuable. In this chapter, we'll take you through the equipment needed for preparing homemade dog food and will focus on basic tools and appliances that help facilitate the cooking process.

Essential Tools for DIY Dog Food

1. Chef's Knife

A high-quality chef's knife is a valuable and crucial tool in the kitchen. It's used for dicing, chopping, and slicing various ingredients, including lean meats, fruits, and vegetables.

Features to Look For:

Sharpness: Always look for a sharp blade that will make cutting more accessible and safer.

Size and Weight: A relaxed size and weight for your hand can decrease fatigue and improve control.

Material: Stainless steel is long-lasting and unaffected by rust.

Usage Tips:

Keep it Sharp: Try to sharpen the blade regularly to sustain efficiency.

Safety First: Your safety matters first. When cutting, use a cutting board and keep your fingers inserted.

2. Cutting board

The cutting board provides the best surface for chopping and dicing ingredients. It helps maintain hygiene and also prevents damage to countertops.

Types:

Wooden Boards: Long-lasting and gentle on knives but need regular maintenance.

Plastic Boards: Easy to wash and dishwasher-safe, but may display knife marks over time.

Usage Tips:

Separate Boards: Use separate boards for vegetables and raw meat to avoid cross-contamination.

Cleaning: Wash with soapy and hot water and clean regularly.

3. Meat Grinder or Food Processor

A food processor and meat grinder are necessary for grinding fish and meat. They are especially useful for mixing ingredients and creating finely minced meat.

Features to Look For:

Capacity: Pick a size that will fit your cooking volume needs.

Attachments: To understand grinding and chopping functions, look for different attachments.

Usage Tips:

Preparation: Cut the meat into smaller slices before processing.

Cleaning: Undo and clean it carefully after each use to avoid bacteria buildup.

4. Mixing Bowls

Mixing bowls are bowls used to combine different ingredients, such as vegetables, meat, and grains. They come in different materials and sizes, such as stainless steel, glass, and plastic.

Features to Look For:

Material: Always choose a material that is easy to clean and works longer. Steel is sturdy and the best for cleaning convenience.

Size Variety: Try to have bowls of different sizes. As it will be helpful for other tasks.

Usage Tips:

Avoid Staining: Use stainless steel or glass to avoid odor and staining.

Stackable: Select bowls that layer together for space-saving storage.

5. Measuring Cups and Spoons

A precise amount of ingredients is essential for balanced nutrition. Measure cups and spoons to ensure you add the accurate amounts of each ingredient.

Features to Look For:

Material: Stainless steel or plastic, with clear markings.

Set Includes: To measure spoons and cups in different sizes for different measurements.

Usage Tips:

Consistency: Use the same measurement tools to maintain consistency in recipes.

Clean Thoroughly: Wash and dry spoons and cups after every measurement to maintain consistency in the future.

6. Food Scale

An analog and digital food scale accurately measures all the ingredients, ensuring proper portion sizes and a balanced meal.

Features to Look For:

Accuracy: Before using a scale, measure it in ounces and grams for versatility.

Capacity: Pick a scale that can handle large weights of batches if needed.

Units: Most digital scales will offer imperial as well as metric units for convenience.

Usage Tips:

Calibrate Regularly: Check and adjust the scale as needed for precision.

Clean Carefully: Clean the scale with a wet cloth, and don't submerge it in water.

7. Blender or Immersion Blender

A blender or immersion blender is useful for making smoothies from vegetables and for cooking grains, fruits, and legumes.

Features to Look For:

Power: You can use the powerful motor to handle more challenging ingredients and make smoother blends.

Attachments: Some blenders have additional attachments for different tasks.

Usage Tips:

Avoid Overloading: To prevent spilling, don't overfill the blender, and make sure to blend.

Clean Immediately: To avoid residue buildup, rinse the blender instantly.

8. Saucepan and Stockpot

Saucepans and stockpots are essential for cooking grains peas, and making soups. They come in several sizes and different kinds of materials.

Features to Look For:

Material: Stainless steel or non-stick options are long-lasting and easy to wash.

Size: Choose sizes built on your typical batch sizes.

Usage Tips:

Use for Multiple Tasks: Stockpots make ample dog food or broth sets.

Monitor Cooking: Stir intermittently to prevent sticking and ensure cooking is even.

9. Roasting Pan and Baking Sheet

Hot pans and baking sheets are used for roasting meats, baking vegetables, and preparing other ingredients.

Features to Look For:

Material: Choose from options like stainless steel, non-stick, or coated surfaces.

Size: Choose a size based on your cooking needs and your oven's capacity.

Usage Tips:

Use Parchment Paper: Line baking sheets with parchment paper to make cleaning easier.

Check Regularly: To prevent any overcooking, monitor cooking duration and temperature.

10. Food Storage Containers

Properly store the prepared dog to keep it fresh and safe. The containers for food storage come in various sizes and materials.

Features to Look For:

Material: To prevent any spoilage, use airtight containers made of glass or plastic

Size: Choose sizes that match your typical batch sizes.

Usage Tips:

Label Containers: Use labels to maintain a record of storage dates and ensure freshness.

Keep Clean: Wash containers entirely before use to avoid contamination.

Having these kitchen tools is necessary to prepare basic recipes for balanced and nutritious homemade dog food. Each tool plays a vital role in ensuring safe and efficient food preparation, from simple tools like chef's knives and cutting boards to particular kinds of food processors and meat grinders. After investing in high-quality and durable equipment cooking healthy and tasty meals for your dog will be a breeze.

Chapter 7

Preservation Methods

Preserving food is the best way to maintain its nutritional value, safety, and freshness. We briefly touched upon refrigerating and freezing before in Chapter 3. Here, we will go through the different methods used for preserving DIY dog food, depending on the plan you have for storing food and the availability of equipment. We'll go over various preservation techniques, including freezing, refrigeration, dehydration, vacuum sealing, and the use of specific preservation tools.

REFRIGERATION

Method

If you want to store your homemade dog food for short-term use, refrigeration is the best method. This method helps slow down bacterial growth and maintains food freshness for a few days.

Steps:

Cool Down: Before placing the food in the refrigerator, please make sure that the cooked dog food is at room temperature so that we can prevent raising the temperature inside the refrigerator.

Portion Out: When the food's temperature drops, divide it into portions that can be consumed easily within a few days.

Store: After dividing the food into eatable portions, place the food in airtight containers or sealable plastic bags. Then you can safely refrigerate.

Duration

Safe Storage Time: This food should be eaten within 3 to 4 days. After this time period, it becomes prone to spoilage.

Tools

Airtight Containers: Use glass or plastic containers with tight lids.

Sealant Bags: Vacuum-sealed or zip-lock bags also help maintain the food's freshness.

Food Thermometer: This thermometer ensures that food has been cooled to a safe temperature before being placed in the refrigerator.

Tips

Label and Date: Mark the containers with preparation dates to track storage time.

Avoid Overloading: Proper air circulation is important in the refrigerator to maintain a consistent temperature. For this purpose, don't overcrowd the refrigerator.

Check Temperature: Make sure the temperature of your refrigerator is 40°F (4°C) or below so that food is safe and fresh.

FREEZING

Method

If you are looking to store homemade food for a long period of time, freezing is the best storage method. It ceases bacterial growth and maintains food quality for a long period of time.

Steps:

Cool Down: Let the food cool down to room temperature before freezing it.

Portion Out: Make food portions into meal size to make defrosting easier.

Pack: After making portions, place the food in freezer-safe bags or containers and remove the air as much as possible.

Duration

Safe Storage Time: Frozen dog food can be stored for 3 to 6 months. After this time period, the food quality might decline, but it will remain safe if placed at a constant temperature.

Tools

Freezer-Safe Containers: Glass and plastic containers designed to maintain freezing temperatures.

Freezer Bags: Certain heavy-duty sealable bags are said to be best for freezing and portioning.

Ice Cube Trays: It helps freeze small amounts of broth.

Tips

Remove Air: Decrease the air exposure to avoid any freezer burn. This is because it can affect food quality.

Label and Date: Use clear labels on each container to maintain a record of food freshness and preparation of contents.

Thaw Safely: To avoid bacterial growth, slow thaw the frozen dog food in the refrigerator overnight instead of at room temperature.

DRYING OR DEHYDRATION

Method

Another method used to store homemade dog food for a longer duration is drying or dehydration. In this method of food storage, drying eradicates moisture from the food, stopping bacterial growth and extending shelf life.

Steps (Equipment-Based)

Preparation: Make slices or dice into equal pieces to ensure even drying.

Dehydrate: Depending on the equipment available, you can dehydrate food using a food dehydrator, oven, or air dry. Each device comes with its set of instructions. Carefully follow the steps.

Cool and Store: Let the dehydrated food cool down completely before storing it in airtight containers.

Steps (Traditional Methods)

Air Drying:

Steps:

1. **Prepare the food**: Cut meat, vegetables, or fruits into thin, uniform slices. This helps them dry evenly.
2. **Lay out the food**: Spread the food in a single layer on a tray or mesh screen. Make sure there is space between pieces for air circulation.
3. **Dry the food**: Place the tray in a warm, dry area with good airflow. You can cover it with a clean cloth or mesh to protect from insects.
4. **Check regularly**: Depending on the humidity and temperature, this process may take a few days. Turn the food every 12 hours to ensure even drying.
5. **Store**: Once the food is fully dry (it should be brittle), store it in an airtight container in a cool, dark place.

Oven Drying:

Steps:

1. **Prepare the food**: Cut meat and vegetables into thin slices or small chunks for even drying.
2. **Set the oven**: Preheat the oven to the lowest possible temperature (usually 60°C/140°F).
3. **Arrange the food**: Place the prepared food on a baking sheet lined with parchment paper. Space them out so they don't touch.
4. **Dry the food**: Place the tray in the oven with the door slightly open to allow moisture to escape. Check the food every 2-3 hours, flipping it midway.
5. **Drying time**: This can take 6-12 hours depending on the food and thickness. The food should be dry and brittle.
6. **Store**: After cooling, store the food in an airtight container.

Duration

Safe Storage Time: Dehydrated dog food or treats can be stored for several months to a year, depending on the storage condition and moisture content.

Tools

Food Dehydrator: This appliance is used to remove moisture from the food efficiently.

Oven: It can help dry by setting it to a low temperature.

Air Drying Racks: Simple racks for dehydrated food in a well-ventilated area.

Tips

Uniform Pieces: Cut food into uniform sizes to ensure even drying.

Store in a Cool, Dry Place: Always dehydrate food in a cool or dry place away from direct sunlight to avoid moisture absorption or growth of bacteria.

Check for Crispness: To avoid mold growth, make sure that food is completely dried before storing.

VACUUM SEALING

Method

Vacuum sealing reduces bacterial growth and oxidation by removing air from the packaging, which helps extend the shelf life of the dog food.

Steps:

1. **Cool Down:** Ensure the food is completely cooled before vacuum sealing.
2. **Portion Out:** Divide food into uniform portions.
3. **Seal:** Place the food in vacuum-seal bags and use a vacuum sealer to eradicate air and seal the bags.

Duration

Safe Storage Time: Vacuum-sealed dog food can be stored in the refrigerator for one week and in the freezer for six to twelve months.

Tools

Vacuum Sealer Machine: This appliance removes air from bags and seals them.

Vacuum-Seal Bags: These are the particular kinds of bags designed to be used with vacuum sealers.

Tips

Ensure a Good Seal: Ensure bags are appropriately sealed to prevent air leaks.

Store Properly: Depending on your storage needs, you can use vacuum-sealed bags that can be stored in the refrigerator or freezer properly.

Label Bags: To keep food fresh and healthy, try using labels marked with dates for easy identification.

VACUUM PRESERVATION (ALTERNATIVE VACUUM-BASED METHODS)

Airtight Containers

Airtight containers are essential for preserving food quality by avoiding air exposure, which can lead to decomposition and loss of nutrients in homemade dog food.

Features to Look For

Material: Use high-quality plastic or glass with tight-fitting lids.

Size: Select sizes based on your typical batch sizes for practical storage.

Tips

Seal Properly: Ensure the lid is sealed tightly to prevent air from entering.

Clean Regularly: Clean containers altogether to avoid contamination.

Freezer Bags

If you are looking for a method to store food for a long time, freezer bags are viable way to go. They are ideal for freezing and portioning homemade dog food.

Features to Look For:

Durability: Use heavy-duty plastic to maintain freezing temperatures.

Sealability: Use the strong seal to avoid air leakage and freezer burn.

Tips:

Remove Air: Before sealing, squeeze the air as much as possible.

Label and Date: To ensure you are using fresh and nutritious food, use label dates to remember it. Mention a label on each bag with the preparation date.

Vacuum Machine

It is a machine that removes air from bags or containers, increasing the shelf life of stored food.

Features to Look For

Power: Look for sufficient suction power to ensure a good seal.

Compatibility: Ensure the machine is well-matched with your vacuum-seal bags or containers.

Tips:

Use Proper Bags: Use bags that are used for vacuum sealing.

Maintain the Machine: To maintain the machine's durability, try following the manufacturer's instructions for maintenance and cleaning.

Food Dehydrator

To create long-lasting treats and save ingredients for a long duration, we use a food dehydrator, which helps remove moisture from the food.

Features to Look For:

Temperature Control: Select a food dehydrator with adjustable settings for various types of food.

Capacity: Select a model with plentiful trays to manage your batch sizes.

Tips

Pre-Treat Food: Certain foods may need pre-treatment (e.g., blanching) before dehydration.

Monitor Drying: Check occasionally to ensure even dehydration and avoid over-drying.

Labels and Markers for Dating

Labels and markers are essential for following preserved food's storage time and contents.

Best Labels and Markers

Waterproof Labels: Labels that can tolerate dampness and freezer conditions.

Permanent Markers: Try to choose permanent markers for writing dates and contents noticeably.

Tips:

Date and Label: Always mention a label on the food with the date of preservation and contents to identify quickly.

Update Labels: If a need arises for repackaging and moving food, then update the label accordingly.

Here's a table that summarize each preservation method we've covered so far:

Preservation Method	Duration	Necessary Tools	Specific Tips
Refrigeration	3-4 days	Airtight containers, labels for dating containers	Divide food into daily portions for easy feeding
Freezing	Up to 3 months	Freezer bags, freezer-safe containers, labels	Freeze food in single portions for easy thawing
Drying or Dehydration	Up to 6 months	Food dehydrator, vacuum-sealed bags, airtight containers	Ensure food is completely dried before storing
Vacuum Sealing	1-2 weeks (fridge), 3-6 months (freezer)	Vacuum sealer, vacuum-sealed bags, labels	Use this method for meat and moist foods to prevent ice crystals

These effective preservation methods are dynamic for sustaining homemade dog food's quality, safety, and nutritional value. By applying techniques such as refrigeration, drying, freezing, and vacuum sealing, along with the appropriate tools, you can ensure that your dog's food remains fresh and safe for intake. Proper storage practices and appropriate equipment will help you provide your dog with healthy and well-preserved meals.

Chapter 8

General Storage Tips

It is necessary to store homemade dog food to maintain its safety, nutritional value, and quality. This chapter explains best storage practices, including portioning, labeling, rotation, and safe defrosting. By following these tips, you can ensure that your dog food remains safe and fresh for intake.

LABELING

Labeling is important for maintaining a record of the freshness of stored dog food. It will help you to know what food is in the refrigerator or freezer, when it was prepared and stored, and by when it needs to be eaten, maintaining its safety and quality.

Key Practices

Date and Content Information

Date of Preparation: Always add the date the food was stored or prepared. This will help you determine how long the food has been stored.

Contents: Always add the cooked food in different containers or bags. This is useful to ensure variety and manage any dietary preferences and changes.

Labeling Tools:

Waterproof Labels: Always use labels that resist moisture and freezer conditions without fading or peeling.

Permanent Markers: Use markers that are resilient to blotting and ensure the text is legible and clear.

Application Tips

Apply Labels Before Freezing: Before freezing or refrigerating the food, attach labels to avoid any mishandling when it might be too sticky or too cold.

Update Labels: When moving the food to another container or repacking, make sure to update the labels accordingly.

PORTIONING

Portioning is very important in terms of storage. It helps manage meal sizes, reduce waste, and ensure that your dog is getting the right amount of food. It is also easier to defrost only what you need rather than a large amount of food.

Key Practices

Determine Portion Size

Based on Dog's Size and Diet: Make portions according to your dog's recommended serving sizes and dietary needs. These vary according to the dog's age, size, and activity level.

Standardize Portions: Use the same portion size consistently to simplify the meal-feeding routines and preparation.

Portioning Tools:

Measuring Cups and Spoons: Use specialized tools to portion out food accurately and consistently.

Food Scale: A food scale can be invaluable for accurate portioning, especially for raw homemade meals

Storage Methods

Single-Serve Bags or Containers: Store individual meal portions in individual bags or containers. This method is especially useful for frozen food.

Vacuum-Sealed Bags:

You can use vacuum sealing to maintain the food's freshness and prevent freezer burn.

SAFE DEFROSTING

Proper defrosting is important to restrict bacterial growth and ensure that food is eatable after thawing.

Key Practices

Thaw in the Refrigerator

Recommended Method: This is the most harmless way to defrost dog food and it keeps the food at a safe temperature as well as inhibit bacterial growth.

Time Needed: Allow enough time for the food to defrost gradually, generally overnight or several hours, depending on the portion size.

Avoid Room Temperature Thawing:

Risk of Bacterial Growth: Defrosting food at room temperature can lead to an unsafe temperature at which bacteria can rapidly multiply.

Emergency Thawing:

If you want to defrost food quickly, use a microwave with a defrost setting, but make sure the food is cooked instantly afterward.

Refrigerate Leftovers:

Immediate Refrigeration: Refrigerate the leftover food immediately after the meal. Don't leave it at room temperature for a longer period of time.

ROTATION

Rotation is a method for moving older food to newer supplies, which helps to prevent waste and ensure that food is completely consumed while remaining fresh. This practice is important for maintaining the ideal safety and quality of different batches over a long period of time.

Key Practices

First In, First out (FIFO)

Principle: Use the first-in, first-out method to feed the oldest food first. Always place the new food ahead of the old food to ensure that the oldest items are eaten first.

Implementation: Check your stored food regularly and adjust the placement to stick to the FIFO.

Regular Inventory Checks

Monitor Storage: Occasionally examine your food inventory to ensure that items are used within their endorsed storage times.

Adjust Portions: Whenever you notice that several types of food are being less used, adjust their portioning size and usage to better manage your supply.

Record Keeping

Track Inventory: Try to maintain a log diary or inventory to keep track of which food is in storage, when it was prepared, and when it is supposed to be finished.

Review Regularly: Keep updating the records as you use them and when you add new food to maintain accurate information about your food supply.

It is mandatory to maintain a proper storage practice by following these guidelines. They are essential for preserving the freshness, safety, and nutrition of the food. When you implement these practices, it will help you maintain consistent and healthy nourishment for your beloved furry companion, so always make sure that your dogs are receiving the best quality.

Chapter 9

Example of Conservation Routine

A well-disciplined conservation routine is important for maintaining the safety, quality and nutritional value of homemade dog food. In this chapter you will be able to get a detailed outline of a conservation routine. This sample routine will explain each step from preparation to rotation and help you successfully manage the supply of your dog food.

SAMPLE ROUTINE FOR COOKING A LARGE BATCH OF DOG FOOD

Steps to Prepare a Large Batch:

1. Plan the Recipe:

Pick a balanced recipe for homemade dog food that includes vegetables, supplements, and grains as desired.

2. Gather Ingredients: Before starting the recipe make sure that all important ingredients and supplies have been gathered.

3. Cook the Food

Preparation: Try to wash peel, chop and wash vegetables. Cut down the meat into manageable pieces.

Cooking: Use suitable cooking methods (boiling, baking, or sautéing) to cook vegetables, grains, and meat. Make sure the food reaches a safe temperature to kill any kind of risky bacteria.

Mixing: Mix all the ingredients comprehensively in a large bowl. If desired use a food processor or blender to get the desired consistency.

4. Cool the Food:

Let the food cool down at room temperature before storing. This will restrict temperature

This restricts the temperature of your refrigerator or freezer to be rising that can also affects the other stored items.

5. Portioning:

Calculate Portions: On the basis of your dog's dietary needs, calculate the suitable daily portion sizes. This can vary depends on the dog size, activity level and age.

Standardize Portions: Use measuring cups or a food scale to make ensure consistency in portion sizes.

Divide the Food: Divide the food into equal portion size depending on the recommended meals for your dog's size.

Portion Out: Use a spoon or scoop to divide the food into separate portions. This will create ease in serving and make sure that each have a balanced nutrition.

5. Use Containers:

Put each portion of food into sealable plastic bags and in airtight containers. Make sure that bags or containers have appropriate size for every meal.

6. Short-Term Storage:

Try to store the week's food in the refrigerator

Container Selection: Before placing the food in the refrigerator use high-quality bags or airtight containers to store the food portions in the refrigerator.

Labeling: Label each container or bag clearly with the date of preparation and contents to maintain the track of freshness.

Storage Location:

Place the containers in the main section of the refrigerator where the temperature is constantly cold (preferably at or below 40°F or 4°C)

Avoid Overcrowding:

Make sure air circulation should be proper around the containers for optimal cooling.

Monitor Storage Time:

Use within a Week: Use the refrigerated food within 3 to 4 days to make sure it remains safe and fresh.

7. Long-Term Storage:

Freeze remaining Portions in Labeled Freezer Bags

Portion Out: Divide the remaining food into meal-sized portions, as described in the portioning section.

Packaging: Place portions into freezer-safe bags or containers. Consider using vacuum-sealed bags to extend shelf life and prevent freezer burn.

Label: Put label on each of the container bag with a date of preparation and the contents. It will help you to maintain a record of what's in the freezer and make sure you use older food meals earlier.

Freezer Placement: Store the labeled bags or containers in the freezer. Make sure they are placed flat initially for better storage and fast freezing.

Monitor Storage Time: The frozen dog food can be stored for 3 to 6 months. After this time period the food will remain safe if placed at constant temperature but the quality might decline.

8. Rotation (with FIFO):

Rotate the refrigerated food and then replace it with new portions from the freezer.

Use Refrigerated Food First: Serve the refrigerated portions of food to your dog before accessing the frozen ones. This will make sure that food in the refrigerator is used up while it is still fresh.

Replace with Frozen Portions: After using the refrigerated portions replace them with defrost portions from the freezer.

Thaw Safely: Place the frozen portions to the refrigerator to defrost overnight. This method make sure that the food stays at a safe temperature and also lessen the risk of bacterial growth.

Refrigerate Leftovers: If any defrost food left then it should be consumed within 1 to 2 days.

9. Update Labels and Inventory:

Track Usage: Check the labels and update your inventory maintain a record of what food is in use and what should be replaced.

Adjust Portions: You can adjust inventory levels and portion sizes according to your dog's storage needs and consumption

To make sure that your cooked batch is still nutritious, fresh and safe for your pet, your perfect routine will include proper preparation, dividing it into portions, storing this food for short-term and long-term storage, and finally rotation using the FIFO method. By implementing these practices, you will be able to maintain a consistent supply of dog food while reducing the waste as well as ensure the optimal well-being and health of your canine.

You're halfway there!

If you found Part 1 helpful and informative, you're going to *love* Part 2!

Now is the time to test your knowledge with quick and easy recipes rich in nutrients.

📚 Get ready to practice like a pro!

Also, if you are enjoying this cookbook, I would really appreciate it if you would leave a review on Amazon. Your feedback is valuable and helps other future nurses find this resource too.

☞ Scan the QR code below and leave a short review!

T

hanks for your help and on to part 2 of this book

Part 3

Basic Recipes

Chapter 10

MEAL PLAN FOR ALL DOG BREEDS

Every breed has unique dietary needs according to its age, size, health status, and activity level. This chapter will provide you a detailed guide to developing meal plans for different dog breeds, including factors to consider and adjustments based on certain requirements.

UNDERSTANDING BREED-SPECIFIC NUTRITIONAL NEEDS

Size and Life Stage:

Small Breeds: Small dogs need food with dense calories as they have higher metabolic rates. The diets rich in nutrients with smaller kibble sizes are mostly preferred.

Medium Breeds: Medium breeds have moderate nutritional needs, but their diet needs to be balanced to maintain optimal health and weight.

Large Breeds: Large breeds of dogs need diets that prevent obesity and support joint health. They also benefit from specially formulated foods that support joint development.

Giant Breeds need food with controlled calorie levels that prevent rapid growth and associated joint issues. They mostly need high-quality proteins and joint supplements.

Puppies need a diet high in fat and protein to support rapid growth and development.

Senior Dogs: Because they have reduced activity levels and a changing metabolism, they need lower-calorie foods with joint support and lower protein.

Activity Level:

Highly Active Dogs: Highly active dogs need a high calorie and protein intake to support their energy needs and maintain their muscles.

Moderately Active Dogs: They need a diet with balanced nutrients and appropriate levels of fats and proteins.

Less Active Dogs: Less active dogs need a controlled calorie intake to avoid weight gain and health issues.

HEALTH CONDITIONS

Allergies: If your dog has any kind of allergy, then hypoallergenic diets or limited-ingredient diets might be necessary.

Diabetes: Dogs with diabetic issues need high-fiber, low-fat diets with controlled carbohydrates to manage their blood sugar levels.

Kidney Disease: Dogs with kidney dysfunctions need low-protein and low-phosphorous diets to help them manage their kidney functions.

CREATING A BALANCED MEAL PLAN

Macronutrients

Protein: Proteins are necessary for muscle development and repair. The sources of protein are eggs, fish, and meat.

Fat: Fats provide energy and also support coat health and skin care. Fish oil and flaxseed are the sources of healthy fats.

Carbohydrates: Carbohydrates are a source of energy and also help with digestion. The best sources of carbohydrates are sweet potatoes, oats, and brown rice.

Micronutrients

Vitamins are crucial for different body functions. A diet with vegetables and fruits that provide vitamins C, E, and A is recommended.

Minerals: Minerals are vital to bone health and overall physiological functioning. They ensure a balanced level of phosphorous, potassium, and calcium.

Hydration

Water: Always provide them with clean and fresh water. Hydration is essential for digestion, overall health, and nutrient absorption.

ADJUSTING MEAL PLANS

Weight Management

Obesity: To reduce weight, keep calorie intake low and increase physical activity. Try to follow a low-calorie diet and have full control over portion size.

Underweight: Use foods high in proteins and fats to increase calorie intake. You can also add supplements to boost calorie density.

Age-Related Adjustments

Puppies: Provide nutrient-rich foods that support growth and development. Follow feeding guidelines specific to puppies.

Seniors: Adjust calorie intake based on activity level. Incorporate joint-supporting supplements and easy-to-digest foods.

Health Conditions

Allergies: Use limited-ingredient diets to identify and avoid allergens.

Kidney Disease: Choose low-protein, low-phosphorus foods and follow dietary recommendations from a veterinarian.

Diabetes: Focus on high-fiber, low-fat foods with controlled carbohydrate levels.

FEEDING PRACTICES

Portion Control

Measuring: Use a measuring cup or scale to ensure accurate portion sizes.

Guidelines: Follow feeding guidelines based on your dog's size, age, and activity level.

Meal Frequency

Puppies: Typically require 3-4 meals per day.

Adult Dogs: Generally do well with two meals per day.

Senior Dogs May benefit from smaller but more frequent meals.

Treats and Snacks

Moderation: Treats should constitute no more than 10% of your dog's daily caloric intake.

Healthy Options: Choose healthy, low-calorie treats and avoid those high in sugars or artificial additives.

To develop a healthy and nutritious diet plan for your dog, understand its needs according to its breed. The following table contains a sample 12-day meal plan that uses recipes from the cookbook section; if you're not sure where to start, give this meal plan a go. For portion sizes, the recipes contain necessary details.

Day	Breakfast	Dinner
1	Chicken and Brown Rice with Carrots	Beef and Sweet Potatoes with Spinach
2	Salmon and Quinoa with Broccoli	Lamb and Brown Rice with Pumpkin
3	Turkey and Oats with Zucchini	Sardines and Sweet Potatoes with Carrots
4	Chicken and Quinoa with Carrots	Trout and Sweet Potatoes with Broccoli
5	Eggs and Oats with Zucchini	Beef and Quinoa with Pumpkin
6	Sardines and Oats with Carrots	Chicken and Sweet Potatoes with Broccoli
7	Eggs and Sweet Potatoes with Carrots	Salmon and Brown Rice with Zucchini
8	Lamb and Sweet Potatoes with Spinach	Trout and Quinoa with Zucchini
9	Beef and Oats with Spinach	Sardines and Brown Rice with Spinach
10	Turkey and Brown Rice with Carrots	Eggs and Brown Rice with Pumpkin
11	Chicken and Oats with Spinach	Beef and Brown Rice with Broccoli
12	Salmon and Spinach with Sweet Potatoes	Lamb and Oats with Carrots

Chapter 11

CHICKEN RECIPES

Chicken Brown Rice with Carrots

Ingredients:

- **Chicken Breast** (boneless and skinless)

Nutritional Values: Rich in lean protein, vitamins B6 and B12, niacin, selenium.

- **Brown Rice**

Nutritional Values: Complex carbohydrates, fiber, B vitamins (B1, B3, B6), magnesium, phosphorus.

- **Carrots**

Nutritional Values: Rich in beta-carotene (vitamin A), vitamin C, vitamin K, fiber.

- **Fish Oil**

Nutritional Values: High concentration of Omega-3 (DHA, EPA), vitamin D.

- **Eggshell Powder**

Nutritional Values: Calcium.

- **Probiotics**

Nutritional Values: Support digestive health.

Amount of Ingredients per Dog Size

Dog Size	Chicken (lbs.)	Brown Rice (cups, uncooked)	Carrots (cups, chopped)	Fish Oil (teaspoons)	Eggshell Powder (teaspoons)	Probiotics (capsules)
Small (up to 11 lbs.)	0.5 lbs.	1/4 cup	1/4 cup	1/2 tsp	1/4 tsp	1/4 capsule
Medium (12-33 lbs.)	1 lbs.	1/2 cup	1/2 cup	1 tsp	1/2 tsp	1/2 capsule
Large (34-66 lbs.)	1.5 lbs.	1 cup	1 cup	2 tsp	1 tsp	1 capsule
Very Large (67-99 lbs.)	2 lbs.	1.5 cups	1.5 cups	3 tsp	1.5 tsp	1.5 capsules
Giant (over 100 lbs.)	2.5 lbs.	2 cups	2 cups	4 tsp	2 tsp	2 capsules

Nutritional Values per Serving (for medium dog, 12-33 lbs.)

- **Calories:** ~300-350 kcal
- **Protein:** ~25-30 g
- **Fat:** ~10-12 g
- **Carbohydrates:** ~25-30 g
- **Fiber:** ~3-4 g
- **Vitamin A:** ~5000 IU
- **Omega-3:** ~500-600 mg

Preparation Times

- Prep: 15 minutes
- Cook: 30 minutes

- Total: 45 minutes

Procedure

1. Cook Brown Rice

- Place rice in a pot with water (1:2 rice to water ratio).
- Bring to a boil, reduce heat and cover.
- Cook for about 30 minutes or until rice is tender.

2: Cook the Chicken

- Place the chicken in a large pot and cover with water.
- Bring to a boil, reduce heat and simmer for about 20 minutes or until cooked through.
- Drain and cut the chicken into bite-sized pieces.

3: Cooking Carrots

- In a pan, cook the carrots with a little water until they are tender (about 10 minutes).

4: Mix Ingredient

- In a large bowl, combine cooked chicken, brown rice, and carrots.
- Add fish oil, eggshell powder, and probiotics.
- Toss well to ensure all ingredients are evenly distributed.

5: Let It Cool

- Let the food cool completely before serving.

Chicken and Sweet Potatoes with Broccoli Recipe

Ingredients

- **Chicken Breast** (boneless and skinless)

Nutritional Values: Rich in lean protein, vitamins B6 and B12, niacin, selenium.

- **Sweet Potatoes**

Nutritional Values: High in beta-carotene (vitamin A), vitamin C, fiber, potassium.

- **Broccoli**

Nutritional Values: Rich in vitamins C and K, fiber, and antioxidants.

- **Fish Oil**

Nutritional Values: High concentration of Omega-3 (DHA, EPA), vitamin D.

- **Eggshell Powder**

Nutritional Values: Calcium.

- **Probiotics**

Nutritional Values: Support digestive health.

Amount of Ingredients per Dog Size

Dog Size	Chicken (lbs.)	Sweet Potatoes (cups, chopped)	Broccoli (cups, chopped)	Fish Oil (teaspoons)	Eggshell Powder (teaspoons)	Probiotics (capsules)
Small (up to 11 lbs.)	0.5 lbs.	1/4 cup	1/4 cup	1/2 tsp	1/4 tsp	1/4 capsule
Medium (12-33 lbs.)	1 lbs.	1/2 cup	1/2 cup	1 tsp	1/2 tsp	1/2 capsule
Large (34-66 lbs.)	1.5 lbs.	1 cup	1 cup	2 tsp	1 tsp	1 capsule
Very Large (67-99 lbs.)	2 lbs.	1.5 cups	1.5 cups	3 tsp	1.5 tsp	1.5 capsules
Giant (over 100 lbs.)	2.5 lbs.	2 cups	2 cups	4 tsp	2 tsp	2 capsules

Nutritional Values per Serving (for medium dog, 12-33 lbs.)

- **Calories**: ~350-400 kcal

- **Protein**: ~30-35 g
- **Fat**: ~12-15 g
- **Carbohydrates**: ~30-35 g
- **Fiber**: ~4-5 g
- **Vitamin A**: ~7000 IU
- **Omega-3**: ~600-700 mg

Preparation Times

- **Prep**: 15 minutes
- **Cook**: 35 minutes
- **Total**: 50 minutes

Procedure

1. Cook Sweet Potatoes

- Peel and chop sweet potatoes. Place them in a pot with water.
- Bring to a boil, reduce heat, and simmer for about 15 minutes or until tender.

2. Cook the Chicken

- Place the chicken in a large pot and cover with water.
- Bring to a boil, reduce heat, and simmer for about 20 minutes or until cooked through.
- Drain and cut the chicken into bite-sized pieces.

3. Cook Broccoli

- In a pan, cook the broccoli with a little water until tender (about 10 minutes).

4. Mix Ingredients

- In a large bowl, combine cooked chicken, sweet potatoes, and broccoli.
- Add fish oil, eggshell powder, and probiotics.
- Toss well to ensure all ingredients are evenly distributed.

5. Let It Cool

- Let the food cool completely before serving.

Chicken and Quinoa with Carrots Recipe

Ingredients:

- **Chicken Breast** (boneless and skinless)

Nutritional Values: Rich in lean protein, vitamins B6 and B12, niacin, selenium.

- **Quinoa**

Nutritional Values: Complete protein, fiber, magnesium, iron.

- **Carrots**

Nutritional Values: Rich in beta-carotene (vitamin A), vitamin C, vitamin K, fiber.

- **Fish Oil**

Nutritional Values: High concentration of Omega-3 (DHA, EPA), vitamin D.

- **Eggshell Powder**

Nutritional Values: Calcium.

- **Probiotics**

Nutritional Values: Support digestive health.

Amount of Ingredients per Dog Size

Dog Size	Chicken (lbs.)	Quinoa (cups, uncooked)	Carrots (cups, chopped)	Fish Oil (teaspoons)	Eggshell Powder (teaspoons)	Probiotics (capsules)
Small (up to 11 lbs.)	0.5 lbs.	1/4 cup	1/4 cup	1/2 tsp	1/4 tsp	1/4 capsule
Medium (12-33 lbs.)	1 lbs.	1/2 cup	1/2 cup	1 tsp	1/2 tsp	1/2 capsule

Large (34-66 lbs.)	1.5 lbs.	1 cup	1 cup	2 tsp	1 tsp	1 capsule
Very Large (67-99 lbs.)	2 lbs.	1.5 cups	1.5 cups	3 tsp	1.5 tsp	1.5 capsules
Giant (over 100 lbs.)	2.5 lbs.	2 cups	2 cups	4 tsp	2 tsp	2 capsules

Nutritional Values per Serving (for medium dog, 12-33 lbs.)

- Calories: ~300-350 kcal
- Protein: ~25-30 g
- Fat: ~10-12 g
- Carbohydrates: ~25-30 g
- Fiber: ~3-4 g
- Vitamin A: ~5000 IU
- Omega-3: ~500-600 mg

Preparation Times

- Prep: 15 minutes
- Cook: 30 minutes
- Total: 45 minutes

Procedure

1. Cook Quinoa

- Rinse quinoa under cold water. Place in a pot with water (1:2 quinoa to water ratio).
- Bring to a boil, reduce heat, cover, and simmer for about 15 minutes or until water is absorbed.

2. Cook the Chicken

- Place the chicken in a large pot and cover with water.
- Bring to a boil, reduce heat, and simmer for about 20 minutes or until cooked through.

- Drain and cut the chicken into bite-sized pieces.

3. Cook Carrots

- In a pan, cook the carrots with a little water until tender (about 10 minutes).

4. Mix Ingredients

- In a large bowl, combine cooked chicken, quinoa, and carrots.
- Add fish oil, eggshell powder, and probiotics.
- Toss well to ensure all ingredients are evenly distributed.

5. Let It Cool

- Let the food cool completely before serving.

Chicken and Oats with Spinach Recipe

Ingredients

- Chicken Breast (boneless and skinless)

Nutritional Values: Rich in lean protein, vitamins B6 and B12, niacin, selenium.

- Oats

Nutritional Values: High in fiber, beta-glucan, vitamins B1 and B5, iron.

- Spinach

Nutritional Values: Rich in vitamins A, C, K, folate, and iron.

- Fish Oil

Nutritional Values: High concentration of Omega-3 (DHA, EPA), vitamin D.

- Eggshell Powder

Nutritional Values: Calcium.

- Probiotics

Nutritional Values: Support digestive health.

Amount of Ingredients per Dog Size

Dog Size	Chicken (lbs.)	Oats (cups, uncooked)	Spinach (cups, chopped)	Fish Oil (teaspoons)	Eggshell Powder (teaspoons)	Probiotics (capsules)
Small (up to 11 lbs.)	0.5 lbs.	1/4 cup	1/4 cup	1/2 tsp	1/4 tsp	1/4 capsule
Medium (12-33 lbs.)	1 lbs.	1/2 cup	1/2 cup	1 tsp	1/2 tsp	1/2 capsule
Large (34-66 lbs.)	1.5 lbs.	1 cup	1 cup	2 tsp	1 tsp	1 capsule
Very Large (67-99 lbs.)	2 lbs.	1.5 cups	1.5 cups	3 tsp	1.5 tsp	1.5 capsules
Giant (over 100 lbs.)	2.5 lbs.	2 cups	2 cups	4 tsp	2 tsp	2 capsules

Nutritional Values per Serving (for medium dog, 12-33 lbs.)

- Calories: ~300-350 kcal
- Protein: ~25-30 g
- Fat: ~10-12 g
- Carbohydrates: ~25-30 g
- Fiber: ~3-4 g
- **Vitamin A**: ~5000 IU
- **Omega-3**: ~500-600 mg

Preparation Times

- **Prep**: 15 minutes
- **Cook**: 30 minutes
- **Total**: 45 minutes

Procedure

1. Cook Oats

- Place oats in a pot with water (1:2 oats to water ratio).
- Bring to a boil, reduce heat, and simmer for about 10 minutes or until oats are tender.

2. Cook the Chicken

- Place the chicken in a large pot and cover with water.
- Bring to a boil, reduce heat, and simmer for about 20 minutes or until cooked through.
- Drain and cut the chicken into bite-sized pieces.

3. Cook Spinach

- In a pan, cook the spinach with a little water until wilted and tender (about 5 minutes).

4. Mix Ingredients

- In a large bowl, combine cooked chicken, oats, and spinach.
- Add fish oil, eggshell powder, and probiotics.
- Toss well to ensure all ingredients are evenly distributed.

5. Let It Cool

- Let the food cool completely before serving.

Chapter 12

BEEF RECIPES

Beef and Sweet Potatoes with Spinach

Ingredients

- **Beef (ground or cubed)**

Nutritional Values: High in protein, iron, zinc, and B vitamins.

- **Sweet Potatoes**

Nutritional Values: High in beta-carotene (vitamin A), vitamin C, fiber, and potassium.

- **Spinach**

Nutritional Values: Rich in vitamins A, C, K, folate, and iron.

- **Fish Oil**

Nutritional Values: High Omega-3 (DHA, EPA) vitamin D concentration.

- **Eggshell Powder**

Nutritional Values: Calcium.

- **Probiotics**

Nutritional Values: Support digestive health.

Amount of Ingredients per Dog Size

Dog Size	Beef (lbs.)	Sweet Potatoes (cups, chopped)	Spinach (cups,	Fish Oil (teaspoons)	Eggshell Powder	Probiotics (capsules)

			chopped)		(teaspoons)	
Small (up to 11 lbs.)	0.5 lbs.	1/4 cup	1/4 cup	1/2 tsp	1/4 tsp	1/4 capsule
Medium (12-33 lbs.)	1 lbs.	1/2 cup	1/2 cup	1 tsp	1/2 tsp	1/2 capsule
Large (34-66 lbs.)	1.5 lbs.	1 cup	1 cup	2 tsp	1 tsp	1 capsule
Very Large (67-99 lbs.)	2 lbs.	1.5 cups	1.5 cups	3 tsp	1.5 tsp	1.5 capsules
Giant (over 100 lbs.)	2.5 lbs.	2 cups	2 cups	4 tsp	2 tsp	2 capsules

Nutritional Values per Serving (for medium dog, 12-33 lbs)

- **Calories**: ~350-400 kcal
- **Protein**: ~30-35 g
- **Fat**: ~12-15 g
- **Carbohydrates**: ~30-35 g
- **Fiber**: ~4-5 g
- **Vitamin A**: ~7000 IU
- **Omega-3**: ~600-700 mg

Preparation Times

- **Prep**: 15 minutes
- **Cook**: 35 minutes
- **Total**: 50 minutes

Procedure

1. Cook Sweet Potatoes

- Peel and chop sweet potatoes. Place in a pot with water.
- Bring to a boil, reduce heat, and simmer for about 15 minutes or until tender.

2. Cook the Beef

- In a pan, cook beef over medium heat until thoroughly browned and cooked through.
- Drain any excess fat.

3. Cook Spinach

- In a separate pan, cook Spinach with a bit of water until it is wilted and tender (about 5 minutes).

4. Mix Ingredients

- Combine cooked beef, sweet potatoes, and Spinach in a large bowl.
- Add fish oil, eggshell powder, and probiotics.
- Toss well to ensure all ingredients are evenly distributed.

5. Let It Cool

- Let the food cool completely before serving.

Beef and Quinoa with Pumpkin

Ingredients

- **Beef (ground or cubed)**

Nutritional Values: High in protein, iron, zinc, and B vitamins.

- **Quinoa**

Nutritional Values: Complete protein, fiber, magnesium, and iron.

- **Pumpkin**

Nutritional Values: High in fiber, beta-carotene (vitamin A), vitamin C, and potassium.

- **Fish Oil**

Nutritional Values: High Omega-3 (DHA, EPA) concentration, vitamin D.

- **Eggshell Powder**

Nutritional Values: Calcium.

- **Probiotics**

Nutritional Values: Support digestive health.

Amount of Ingredients per Dog Size

Dog Size	Beef (lbs.)	Quinoa (cups, uncooked)	Pumpkin (cups, chopped)	Fish Oil (teaspoons)	Eggshell Powder (teaspoons)	Probiotics (capsules)
Small (up to 11 lbs.)	0.5 lbs.	1/4 cup	1/4 cup	1/2 tsp	1/4 tsp	1/4 capsule
Medium (12-33 lbs.)	1 lbs.	1/2 cup	1/2 cup	1 tsp	1/2 tsp	1/2 capsule
Large (34-66 lbs.)	1.5 lbs.	1 cup	1 cup	2 tsp	1 tsp	1 capsule
Very Large (67-99 lbs.)	2 lbs.	1.5 cups	1.5 cups	3 tsp	1.5 tsp	1.5 capsules
Giant (over 100 lbs.)	2.5 lbs.	2 cups	2 cups	4 tsp	2 tsp	2 capsules

Nutritional Values per Serving (for medium dog, 12-33 lbs)

- **Calories**: ~300-350 kcal
- **Protein**: ~25-30 g
- **Fat**: ~10-12 g
- **Carbohydrates**: ~25-30 g
- **Fiber**: ~3-4 g
- **Vitamin A**: ~5000 IU
- **Omega-3**: ~500-600 mg

Preparation Times

- **Prep**: 15 minutes
- **Cook**: 35 minutes

- **Total**: 50 minutes

Procedure

1. Cook Quinoa

- Rinse Quinoa under cold water. Place in a pot with water (1:2 Quinoa to water ratio). Bring to a boil, reduce heat, cover, and simmer for about 15 minutes or until water is absorbed.

2. Cook the beef

- Cook the beef in a pan, cooking it over medium heat until thoroughly browned and cooked. Drain any excess fat.

3. Cook Pumpkin

- Peel and chop pumpkin. Place in a pot with water. Bring to a boil, reduce heat, and simmer for about 15 minutes or until tender.

4. Mix Ingredients

- Combine cooked beef, Quinoa, and pumpkin in a large bowl. Add fish oil, eggshell powder, and probiotics. Toss well to ensure all ingredients are evenly distributed.

5. Let It Cool

- Let the food cool completely before serving.

Beef and Oats with Spinach

Ingredients

- **Beef (ground or cubed)**

Nutritional Values: High in protein, iron, zinc, and B vitamins.

- **Oats**

Nutritional Values: High in fiber, beta-glucan, vitamins B1 and B5, and iron.

- **Spinach**

Nutritional Values: Rich in vitamins A, C, K, folate, and iron.

- **Fish Oil**

Nutritional Values: High Omega-3 (DHA, EPA) concentration, vitamin D.

- **Eggshell Powder**

Nutritional Values: Calcium.

- **Probiotics**

Nutritional Values: Support digestive health.

Amount of Ingredients per Dog Size

Dog Size	Beef (lbs.)	Oats (cups, uncooked)	Spinach (cups, chopped)	Fish Oil (teaspoons)	Eggshell Powder (teaspoons)	Probiotics (capsules)
Small (up to 11 lbs.)	0.5 lbs.	1/4 cup	1/4 cup	1/2 tsp	1/4 tsp	1/4 capsule
Medium (12-33 lbs.)	1 lbs.	1/2 cup	1/2 cup	1 tsp	1/2 tsp	1/2 capsule
Large (34-66 lbs.)	1.5 lbs.	1 cup	1 cup	2 tsp	1 tsp	1 capsule
Very Large (67-99 lbs.)	2 lbs.	1.5 cups	1.5 cups	3 tsp	1.5 tsp	1.5 capsules
Giant (over 100 lbs.)	2.5 lbs.	2 cups	2 cups	4 tsp	2 tsp	2 capsules

Nutritional Values per Serving (for medium dog, 12-33 lbs)

- **Calories**: ~300-350 kcal
- **Protein**: ~25-30 g
- **Fat**: ~10-12 g
- **Carbohydrates**: ~25-30 g

- **Fiber**: ~3-4 g
- **Vitamin A**: ~5000 IU
- **Omega-3**: ~500-600 mg

Preparation Times

- **Prep**: 15 minutes
- **Cook**: 30 minutes
- **Total**: 45 minutes

Procedure

1. Cook Oats

- Place oats in a pot with water (1:2 oats to water ratio).
- Bring to a boil, reduce heat, and simmer for 10 minutes or until tender.

2. Cook the Beef

- In a pan, cook beef over medium heat until thoroughly browned and cooked through. Drain any excess fat.

3. Cook Spinach

- In a separate pan, cook Spinach with a bit of water until it is wilted and tender (about 5 minutes).

4. Mix Ingredients

- In a large bowl, combine cooked beef, oats, and Spinach. Add fish oil, eggshell powder, and probiotics. Toss well to ensure all ingredients are evenly distributed.

5. Let It Cool

- Let the food cool completely before serving.

Beef and Brown Rice with Broccoli

Ingredients

- **Beef (ground or cubed)**

Nutritional Values: High in protein, iron, zinc, and B vitamins.

- **Brown Rice**

Nutritional Values: Complex carbohydrates, fiber, B vitamins (B1, B3, B6), magnesium, phosphorus.

- **Broccoli**

Nutritional Values: Rich in vitamins C, K, and A, fiber, and antioxidants.

- **Fish Oil**

Nutritional Values: High Omega-3 (DHA, EPA) concentration, vitamin D.

- **Eggshell Powder**

Nutritional Values: Calcium.

- **Probiotics**

Nutritional Values: Support digestive health.

Amount of Ingredients per Dog Size

Dog Size	Beef (lbs.)	Brown Rice (cups, uncooked)	Broccoli (cups, chopped)	Fish Oil (teaspoons)	Eggshell Powder (teaspoons)	Probiotics (capsules)
Small (up to 11 lbs.)	0.5 lbs.	1/4 cup	1/4 cup	1/2 tsp	1/4 tsp	1/4 capsule
Medium (12-33 lbs.)	1 lbs.	1/2 cup	1/2 cup	1 tsp	1/2 tsp	1/2 capsule
Large (34-66 lbs.)	1.5 lbs.	1 cup	1 cup	2 tsp	1 tsp	1 capsule
Very Large (67-99 lbs.)	2 lbs.	1.5 cups	1.5 cups	3 tsp	1.5 tsp	1.5 capsules
Giant	2.5 lbs.	2 cups	2 cups	4 tsp	2 tsp	2 capsules

(over 100 lbs.)						

Nutritional Values per Serving (for medium dog, 12-33 lbs)

- **Calories**: 350-400 kcal
- **Protein**: 30-35 g
- **Fat**: 12-15 g
- **Carbohydrates**: 30-35 g
- **Fiber**: 4-5 g
- **Vitamin A**: 5000 IU
- **Omega-3**: 600-700 mg

Preparation Times

- **Prep**: 15 minutes
- **Cook**: 35 minutes
- **Total**: 50 minutes

Procedure

1. Cook Brown Rice

- Place rice in a pot with water (1:2 rice to water ratio).
- Bring to a boil, reduce heat, and cover.
- Cook for about 30 minutes or until tender.

2. Cook the Beef

- In a pan, cook beef over medium heat until thoroughly browned and cooked through.
- Drain any excess fat.

3. Cook Broccoli

- In a separate pan, steam or boil broccoli until tender (about 5-10 minutes).

4. Mix Ingredients

- Combine cooked beef, brown rice, and broccoli in a large bowl.
- Add fish oil, eggshell powder, and probiotics.
- Toss well to ensure all ingredients are evenly distributed.

5. Let It Cool

- Let the food cool completely before serving.

Chapter 13

LAMB RECIPES

Lamb and Brown Rice with Pumpkin

Ingredients

- **Lamb (ground or cubed)**

Nutritional Values: High in protein, iron, zinc, and B vitamins.

- **Brown Rice**

Nutritional Values: Complex carbohydrates, fiber, B vitamins (B1, B3, B6), magnesium, phosphorus.

- **Pumpkin**

Nutritional Values: High in fiber, beta-carotene (vitamin A), vitamin C, and potassium.

- **Fish Oil**

Nutritional Values: High Omega-3 (DHA, EPA) concentration, vitamin D.

- **Eggshell Powder**

Nutritional Values: Calcium.

- **Probiotics**
- **Nutritional Values:** Support digestive health.

Amount of Ingredients per Dog Size

Dog Size	Lamb (lbs.)	Brown Rice (cups, uncooked)	Pumpkin (cups, chopped)	Fish Oil (teaspoons)	Eggshell Powder (teaspoons)	Probiotics (capsules)
Small (up to 11 lbs.)	0.5 lbs.	1/4 cup	1/4 cup	1/2 tsp	1/4 tsp	1/4 capsule
Medium (12-33 lbs.)	1 lbs.	1/2 cup	1/2 cup	1 tsp	1/2 tsp	1/2 capsule
Large (34-66 lbs.)	1.5 lbs.	1 cup	1 cup	2 tsp	1 tsp	1 capsule
Very Large (67-99 lbs.)	2 lbs.	1.5 cups	1.5 cups	3 tsp	1.5 tsp	1.5 capsules
Giant (over 100 lbs.)	2.5 lbs.	2 cups	2 cups	4 tsp	2 tsp	2 capsules

Nutritional Values per Serving (for medium dog, 12-33 lbs)

- **Calories:** 350-400 kcal
- **Protein:** 30-35 g
- **Fat:** 12-15 g
- **Carbohydrates:** 30-35 g
- **Fiber:** 4-5 g
- **Vitamin A:** 5000 IU
- **Omega-3:** 600-700 mg

Preparation Times

- Prep: 15 minutes
- Cook: 35 minutes
- Total: 50 minutes

Procedure

1. Cook Brown Rice

- Place rice in a pot with water (1:2 rice to water ratio).
- Bring to a boil, reduce heat, and cover.
- Cook for about 30 minutes or until tender.

2. Cook the Lamb

- In a pan, cook lamb over medium heat until thoroughly browned and cooked through. Drain any excess fat.

3. Cook Pumpkin

- Peel and chop pumpkin. Place in a pot with water. Bring to a boil, reduce heat, and simmer for about 15 minutes or until tender.

4. Mix ingredients

- Mix cooked lamb, brown rice, and Pumpkin in a large bowl. Add fish oil, eggshell powder, and probiotics. Toss well to ensure all ingredients are evenly distributed.

5. Let It Cool

- Let the food cool completely before serving.

Lamb and Sweet Potatoes with Spinach

Ingredients

- **Lamb (ground or cubed)**

Nutritional Values: High in protein, iron, zinc, and B vitamins.

- **Sweet Potatoes**

Nutritional Values: High in beta-carotene (vitamin A), vitamin C, fiber, and potassium.

- **Spinach**

Nutritional Values: Rich in vitamins A, C, K, folate, and iron.

- **Fish Oil**

Nutritional Values: High Omega-3 (DHA, EPA) concentration, vitamin D.

- **Eggshell Powder**

Nutritional Values: Calcium.

- **Probiotics**

Nutritional Values: Support digestive health.

Amount of Ingredients per Dog Size

Dog Size	Lamb (lbs.)	Sweet Potatoes (cups, chopped)	Spinach (cups, chopped)	Fish Oil (teaspoons)	Eggshell Powder (teaspoons)	Probiotics (capsules)
Small (up to 11 lbs.)	0.5 lbs.	1/4 cup	1/4 cup	1/2 tsp	1/4 tsp	1/4 capsule
Medium (12-33 lbs.)	1 lbs.	1/2 cup	1/2 cup	1 tsp	1/2 tsp	1/2 capsule
Large (34-66 lbs.)	1.5 lbs.	1 cup	1 cup	2 tsp	1 tsp	1 capsule
Very Large (67-99 lbs.)	2 lbs.	1.5 cups	1.5 cups	3 tsp	1.5 tsp	1.5 capsules
Giant (over 100 lbs.)	2.5 lbs.	2 cups	2 cups	4 tsp	2 tsp	2 capsules

Nutritional Values per Serving (for medium dog, 12-33 lbs)

- **Calories**: 350-400 kcal
- **Protein**: 30-35 g
- **Fat**: 12-15 g
- **Carbohydrates**: 30-35 g
- **Fiber**: 4-5 g
- **Vitamin A**: 7000 IU
- **Omega-3**: 600-700 mg

Preparation Times

- **Prep**: 15 minutes
- **Cook**: 35 minutes
- **Total**: 50 minutes

Procedure

1. Cook Sweet Potatoes

- Peel and chop sweet potatoes. Place in a pot with water.
- Bring to a boil, reduce heat, and simmer for about 15 minutes or until tender.

2. Cook the Lamb

- In a pan, cook lamb over medium heat until thoroughly browned and cooked through.
- Drain any excess fat.

3. Cook Spinach

- In a separate pan, cook spinach with water until wilted and tender (about 5 minutes).

4. Mix Ingredients

- Combine cooked lamb, sweet potatoes, and spinach in a large bowl.
- Add fish oil, eggshell powder, and probiotics.
- Toss well to ensure all ingredients are evenly distributed.

5. Let It Cool

- Let the food cool completely before serving.

Lamb and Oats with Carrots

Ingredients

- **Lamb (ground or cubed)**

Nutritional Values: High in protein, iron, zinc, and B vitamins.

- **Oats**

Nutritional Values: High in fiber, beta-glucan, vitamins B1 and B5, and iron.

- **Carrots**

Nutritional Values: Rich in beta-carotene (vitamin A), vitamin C, K, and fiber.

- **Fish Oil**

Nutritional Values: High Omega-3 (DHA, EPA) concentration, vitamin D.

- **Eggshell Powder**

Nutritional Values: Calcium.

- **Probiotics**

Nutritional Values: Support digestive health.

Amount of Ingredients per Dog Size

Dog Size	Lamb (lbs.)	Oats (cups, uncooked)	Carrots (cups, chopped)	Fish Oil (teaspoons)	Eggshell Powder (teaspoons)	Probiotics (capsules)
Small (up to 11 lbs.)	0.5 lbs.	1/4 cup	1/4 cup	1/2 tsp	1/4 tsp	1/4 capsule
Medium (12-33 lbs.)	1 lbs.	1/2 cup	1/2 cup	1 tsp	1/2 tsp	1/2 capsule
Large (34-66 lbs.)	1.5 lbs.	1 cup	1 cup	2 tsp	1 tsp	1 capsule
Very Large (67-99 lbs.)	2 lbs.	1.5 cups	1.5 cups	3 tsp	1.5 tsp	1.5 capsules
Giant (over 100 lbs.)	2.5 lbs.	2 cups	2 cups	4 tsp	2 tsp	2 capsules

Nutritional Values per Serving (for medium dog, 12-33 lbs)

- **Calories:** 300-350 kcal

- **Protein:** 25-30 g
- **Fat:** 10-12 g
- **Carbohydrates:** 25-30 g
- **Fiber:** 3-4 g
- **Vitamin A:** 5000 IU
- **Omega-3:** 500-600 mg

Preparation Times

- · Prep: 15 minutes
- · Cook: 30 minutes
- · Total: 45 minutes

Procedure

1. Cook Oats

- Place oats in a pot with water (1:2 oats to water ratio).
- Bring to a boil, reduce heat, and simmer for 10 minutes or until tender.

2. Cook the Lamb

- In a pan, cook lamb over medium heat until thoroughly browned and cooked through.
- Drain any excess fat.

3. Cook Carrots

- In a separate pan, cook carrots with some water until tender (about 10 minutes).

4. Mix Ingredients

- In a large bowl, combine cooked lamb, oats, and carrots.
- Add fish oil, eggshell powder, and probiotics.
- Toss well to ensure all ingredients are evenly distributed.

5. Let It Cool

- Let the food cool completely before serving.

Chapter 14

Turkey Recipes

Turkey and Oats with Zucchini

Ingredients

- **Turkey**

Nutritional Values: High protein, vitamins B6 and B12, niacin, selenium, and zinc.

- **Oats**

Nutritional Values: Rich in fiber, vitamins B1 and B5, iron, magnesium, and antioxidants.

- **Zucchini**

Nutritional Values: Low in calories, high in vitamin C, vitamin A, potassium, and fibre.

- **Fish Oil**

Nutritional Values: High Omega-3 (DHA, EPA) concentration, vitamin D.

- **Eggshell Powder**

Nutritional Values: Calcium.

- **Probiotics**

Nutritional Values: Support digestive health.

Amount of Ingredients per Dog Size

Dog Size	Turkey (cups, cooked)	Oats (cups)	Zucchini (cups, chopped)	Fish Oil (teaspoons)	Eggshell Powder (teaspoons)	Probiotics (capsules)
Small (up to 11 lbs)	1/2 cup	1/4 cup	1/4 cup	1/2 tsp	1/4 tsp	1/4 capsule
Medium (12-33 lbs)	1 cup	1/2 cup	1/2 cup	1 tsp	1/2 tsp	1/2 capsule
Large (34-66 lbs)	1.5 cups	1 cup	1 cup	2 tsp	1 tsp	1 capsule
Very Large (67-99 lbs)	2 cups	1.5 cups	1.5 cups	3 tsp	1.5 tsp	1.5 capsules
Giant (over 100 lbs)	3 cups	2 cups	2 cups	4 tsp	2 tsp	2 capsules

Nutritional Values per Serving (for medium dog, 12-33 lbs)

- **Calories:** ~350-400 kcal
- **Protein:** ~25-30 g
- **Fat:** ~15-20 g
- **Carbohydrates:** ~25-30 g
- **Fiber:** ~5-6 g
- **Vitamin A:** ~2000 IU
- **Omega-3:** ~400-500 mg

Preparation Times

- Prep: 10 minutes
- Cook: 25 minutes

- Total: 35 minutes

Procedure

1. Cook Turkey

- Cook ground turkey in a pan until entirely done (about 10 minutes).
- Drain any excess fat.

2. Cook Oats

- Boil the water in a Bowl.
- Add oats and reduce heat, cooking until soft (about 5 minutes).
- Let cool slightly.

3. Prepare Zucchini

- In a separate pan, cook zucchini with a bit of water until tender (about 10 minutes).

4. Combine Ingredients

- In a large bowl, mix cooked turkey, oats, and zucchini.
- Add fish oil, eggshell powder, and probiotics.
- Toss well to ensure all ingredients are evenly distributed.

5. Let It Cool

- Let the food cool completely before serving.

Turkey and Brown Rice with Carrots

Ingredients

- **Turkey**

Nutritional Values: High protein, vitamins B6 and B12, niacin, selenium, and zinc.

- **Brown Rice**

Nutritional Values: High in fiber, magnesium, manganese, and B vitamins.

- **Carrots**

Nutritional Values: Rich in beta-carotene (vitamin A), vitamin C, K, and fiber.

- **Fish Oil**

Nutritional Values: High Omega-3 (DHA, EPA) concentration, vitamin D.

- **Eggshell Powder**

Nutritional Values: Calcium.

- **Probiotics**

Nutritional Values: Support digestive health.

Amount of Ingredients per Dog Size

Dog Size	Turkey (cups, cooked)	Brown Rice (cups, cooked)	Carrots (cups, chopped)	Fish Oil (teaspoons)	Eggshell Powder (teaspoons)	Probiotics (capsules)
Small (up to 11 lbs)	1/2 cup	1/4 cup	1/4 cup	1/2 tsp	1/4 tsp	1/4 capsule
Medium (12-33 lbs)	1 cup	1/2 cup	1/2 cup	1 tsp	1/2 tsp	1/2 capsule
Large (34-66 lbs)	1.5 cups	1 cup	1 cup	2 tsp	1 tsp	1 capsule
Very Large (67-99 lbs)	2 cups	1.5 cups	1.5 cups	3 tsp	1.5 tsp	1.5 capsules
Giant (over 100 lbs)	3 cups	2 cups	2 cups	4 tsp	2 tsp	2 capsules

Nutritional Values per Serving (for medium dog, 12-33 lbs)

- **Calories:** ~350-400 kcal
- **Protein:** ~25-30 g
- **Fat:** ~15-20 g

- **Carbohydrates:** ~30-35 g
- **Fiber:** ~5-6 g
- **Vitamin A**: ~5000 IU
- **Omega-3:** ~400-500 mg

Preparation Times

- Prep: 10 minutes
- Cook: 30 minutes
- Total: 40 minutes

Procedure

1. Cook Turkey

- Cook ground turkey in a pan until entirely done (about 10 minutes).
- Drain any excess fat.

2. Cook Brown Rice

- Let the water boil in a pot.
- Add brown rice and reduce heat, cooking until tender (about 20-25 minutes).
- Let cool slightly.

3. Prepare Carrots

- In a separate pan, cook carrots with water until tender (about 10 minutes).

4. Combine Ingredients

- Mix cooked turkey, brown rice, and carrots in a large bowl.
- Add fish oil, eggshell powder, and probiotics.
- Toss well to ensure all ingredients are evenly distributed.

5. Let It Cool

- Let the food cool completely before serving.

Chapter 15

Salmon Recipes

Salmon and Quinoa with Broccoli

Ingredients

- **Salmon (fresh or frozen, boneless and skinless)**

Nutritional Values: Rich in Omega-3 fatty acids (DHA, EPA), protein, vitamins B12 and D, and selenium.

- **Quinoa**

Nutritional Values: Complete protein, high in fiber, B vitamins (B1, B2, B6), magnesium, phosphorus.

- **Broccoli**

Nutritional Values: Rich in vitamins C, K, and A, fiber, and antioxidants.

- **Fish Oil**

Nutritional Values: High Omega-3 (DHA, EPA) concentration and vitamin D.

- **Eggshell Powder**

Nutritional Values: Calcium.

- **Probiotics**

Nutritional Values: Support digestive health.

Amount of Ingredients per Dog Size

Dog Size	Salmon (lbs.)	Quinoa (cups, uncooked)	Broccoli (cups, chopped)	Fish Oil (teaspoons)	Eggshell Powder (teaspoons)	Probiotics (capsules)
Small (up to 11 lbs)	0.5 lbs	1/4 cup	1/4 cup	1/2 tsp	1/4 tsp	1/4 capsule
Medium (12-33 lbs)	1 lbs	1/2 cup	1/2 cup	1 tsp	1/2 tsp	1/2 capsule
Large (34-66 lbs)	1.5 lbs	1 cup	1 cup	2 tsp	1 tsp	1 capsule
Very Large (67-99 lbs)	2 lbs	1.5 cups	1.5 cups	3 tsp	1.5 tsp	1.5 capsules
Giant (over 100 lbs)	2.5 lbs	2 cups	2 cups	4 tsp	2 tsp	2 capsules

Nutritional Values per Serving (for medium dog, 12-33 lbs)

- **Calories**: 350-400 kcal
- **Protein**: 30-35 g
- **Fat**: 15-18 g
- **Carbohydrates**: 30-35 g

- **Fiber**: 4-5 g
- **Vitamin A**: 5000 IU
- **Omega-3**: 600-700 mg

Preparation Times

- **Prep**: 15 minutes
- **Cook**: 30 minutes
- **Total**: 45 minutes

Procedure

1. Cook Quinoa

- Place quinoa in a pot with water (1:2 quinoa to water ratio).
- Bring to a boil, reduce heat, and cover.
- Cook for about 15 minutes or until quinoa is tender and water is absorbed.

2. Cook the Salmon

- In a pan, cook salmon over medium heat until fully cooked (about 10 minutes).
- Flake the salmon into bite-sized pieces and remove any bones.

3. Cook Broccoli

- Steam or boil Broccoli until tender (about 5-10 minutes).

4. Mix Ingredients

- In a large bowl, combine cooked salmon, quinoa, and Broccoli.
- Add fish oil, eggshell powder, and probiotics.
- Toss well to ensure all ingredients are evenly distributed.

5. Let It Cool

- Let the food cool completely before serving.

Salmon and Brown Rice with Zucchini

Ingredients

- **Salmon (fresh or frozen, boneless and skinless)**

Nutritional Values: Rich in Omega-3 fatty acids (DHA, EPA), protein, vitamins B12 and D, and selenium.

- **Brown Rice**

Nutritional Values: Complex carbohydrates, fiber, B vitamins (B1, B3, B6), magnesium, phosphorus.

- **Zucchini**

Nutritional Values: Low in calories, high in vitamins C and A, fiber.

- **Fish Oil**

Nutritional Values: High Omega-3 (DHA, EPA) concentration and vitamin D.

- **Eggshell Powder**

Nutritional Values: Calcium.

- **Probiotics**

Nutritional Values: Support digestive health.

Amount of Ingredients per Dog Size

Dog Size	Salmon (lbs)	Brown Rice (cups, uncooked)	Zucchini (cups, chopped)	Fish Oil (teaspoons)	Eggshell Powder (teaspoons)	Probiotics (capsules)
Small (up to 11 lbs)	0.5 lbs	1/4 cup	1/4 cup	1/2 tsp	1/4 tsp	1/4 capsule
Medium (12-33 lbs)	1 lbs	1/2 cup	1/2 cup	1 tsp	1/2 tsp	1/2 capsule
Large (34-66 lbs)	1.5 lbs	1 cup	1 cup	2 tsp	1 tsp	1 capsule
Very Large	2 lbs	1.5 cups	1.5 cups	3 tsp	1.5 tsp	1.5 capsules

(67-99 lbs)						
Giant (over 100 lbs)	2.5 lbs	2 cups	2 cups	4 tsp	2 tsp	2 capsules

Nutritional Values per Serving (for medium dog, 12-33 lbs)

- · **Calories**: 300-350 kcal
- · **Protein**: 25-30 g
- · **Fat**: 10-12 g
- · **Carbohydrates**: 25-30 g
- · **Fiber**: 3-4 g
- · **Vitamin A**: 4000 IU
- · **Omega-3**: 500-600 mg

Preparation Times

- · **Prep**: 15 minutes
- · **Cook**: 30 minutes
- · **Total**: 45 minutes

Procedure

1. Cook Brown Rice

- Place rice in a pot with water (1:2 rice to water ratio).
- Bring to a boil, reduce heat, and cover.
- Cook for about 30 minutes or until tender.

2. Cook the Salmon

- In a pan, cook salmon over medium heat until fully cooked (about 10 minutes).
- Flake the salmon into bite-sized pieces and remove any bones.

3. Cook Zucchini

- In a separate pan, cook Zucchini with a bit of water until tender (about 5-7 minutes).

4. Mix Ingredients

- Combine cooked salmon, brown rice, and zucchini in a large bowl.
- Add fish oil, eggshell powder, and probiotics.
- Toss well to ensure all ingredients are evenly distributed.

5. Let It Cool

- Let the food cool completely before serving.

Salmon and Spinach with Sweet Potatoes

Ingredients

- **Salmon (fresh or frozen, boneless and skinless)**

Nutritional Values: Rich in Omega-3 fatty acids (DHA, EPA), protein, vitamins B12 and D, and selenium.

- **Spinach**

Nutritional Values: Rich in vitamins A, C, K, folate, and iron.

- **Sweet Potatoes**

Nutritional Values: High in beta-carotene (vitamin A), vitamin C, fiber, and potassium.

- **Fish Oil**

Nutritional Values: High Omega-3 (DHA, EPA) concentration, vitamin D.

- **Eggshell Powder**

Nutritional Values: Calcium.

- **Probiotics**

Nutritional Values: Support digestive health.

Amount of Ingredients per Dog Size

Dog Size	Salmon (lbs.)	Spinach (cups, chopped)	Sweet Potatoes (cups, chopped)	Fish Oil (teaspoons)	Eggshell Powder (teaspoons)	Probiotics (capsules)
Small (up to 11 lbs.)	0.5 lbs.	1/4 cup	1/4 cup	1/2 tsp	1/4 tsp	1/4 capsule
Medium (12-33 lbs.)	1 lbs.	1/2 cup	1/2 cup	1 tsp	1/2 tsp	1/2 capsule
Large (34-66 lbs.)	1.5 lbs.	1 cup	1 cup	2 tsp	1 tsp	1 capsule
Very Large (67-99 lbs.)	2 lbs.	1.5 cups	1.5 cups	3 tsp	1.5 tsp	1.5 capsules
Giant (over 100 lbs.)	2.5 lbs.	2 cups	2 cups	4 tsp	2 tsp	2 capsules

Nutritional Values per Serving (for medium dog, 12-33 lbs)

- **Calories**: ~350-400 kcal
- **Protein**: ~30-35 g
- **Fat**: ~15-18 g
- **Carbohydrates**: ~30-35 g
- **Fiber**: ~4-5 g
- **Vitamin A**: ~6000 IU
- **Omega-3**: ~700-800 mg

Preparation Times

- **Prep**: 15 minutes
- **Cook**: 30 minutes
- **Total**: 45 minutes

Procedure

1. Cook Sweet Potatoes

- Place sweet potatoes in a pot with water.
- Bring to a boil, reduce heat, and cook until tender (about 20 minutes).
- Drain and mash.

2. Cook the Salmon

- In a pan, cook salmon over medium heat until fully cooked (about 10 minutes).
- Flake the salmon into bite-sized pieces and remove any bones.

3. Cook Spinach

- In a separate pan, cook spinach with water until wilted (about 3-5 minutes).

4. Mix Ingredients

- Combine cooked salmon, sweet potatoes, and spinach in a large bowl.
- Add fish oil, eggshell powder, and probiotics.
- Toss well to ensure all ingredients are evenly distributed.

5. Let It Cool

- Let the food cool completely before serving.

Chapter 16

SARDINE RECIPES

Sardines and Sweet Potatoes with Carrots

Ingredients

- · **Sardines (canned in water, boneless and skinless)**

Nutritional Values: High in Omega-3 fatty acids (DHA, EPA), protein, vitamins B12 and D, calcium.

- · **Sweet Potatoes**

Nutritional Values: High in beta-carotene (vitamin A), vitamin C, fiber, and potassium.

- · **Carrots**

Nutritional Values: Rich in beta-carotene (vitamin A), vitamin C, K, and fiber.

- · **Fish Oil**

Nutritional Values: High Omega-3 (DHA, EPA) vitamin D concentration.

- · **Eggshell Powder**

Nutritional Values: Calcium.

- · **Probiotics**

Nutritional Values: Support digestive health.

Amount of Ingredients per Dog Size

Dog Size	Sardines (cans)	Sweet Potatoes (cups, chopped)	Carrots (cups, chopped)	Fish Oil (teaspoons)	Eggshell Powder (teaspoons)	Probiotics (capsules)
Small (up to 11 lbs.)	1/2 can	1/4 cup	1/4 cup	1/2 tsp	1/4 tsp	1/4 capsule
Medium (12-33 lbs.)	1 can	1/2 cup	1/2 cup	1 tsp	1/2 tsp	1/2 capsule
Large (34-66 lbs.)	1.5 cans	1 cup	1 cup	2 tsp	1 tsp	1 capsule
Very Large (67-99 lbs.)	2 cans	1.5 cups	1.5 cups	3 tsp	1.5 tsp	1.5 capsules
Giant (over 100 lbs.)	2.5 cans	2 cups	2 cups	4 tsp	2 tsp	2 capsules

Nutritional Values per Serving (for medium dog, 12-33 lbs.)

- **Calories**: ~300-350 kcal
- **Protein**: ~25-30 g
- **Fat**: ~15-20 g
- **Carbohydrates**: ~25-30 g
- **Fiber**: ~4-5 g
- **Vitamin A**: ~6000 IU
- **Omega-3**: ~700-800 mg

Preparation Times

- **Prep**: 15 minutes
- **Cook**: 20 minutes
- **Total**: 35 minutes

Procedure

1. Cook Sweet Potatoes

- Place sweet potatoes in a pot with water.
- Bring to a boil, reduce heat, and cook until tender (about 20 minutes).
- Drain and mash.

2. Prepare Carrots

- In a pan, cook carrots with some water until tender (about 10 minutes).

3. Combine Ingredients

- Mix the canned sardines (drained), mashed sweet potatoes, and cooked carrots in a large bowl.
- Add fish oil, eggshell powder, and probiotics.
- Toss well to ensure all ingredients are evenly distributed.

4. Let It Cool

- Let the food cool completely before serving.

Sardines and Oats with Carrots

Ingredients

- **Sardines (canned in water, boneless, and skinless)**

Nutritional Values: High in Omega-3 fatty acids (DHA, EPA), protein, vitamins B12 and D, and calcium.

- **Oats**

Nutritional Values: High in fiber, protein, B vitamins (B1, B5), iron, and magnesium.

- **Carrots**

Nutritional Values: Rich in beta-carotene (vitamin A), vitamin C, K, and fiber.

- **Fish Oil**

Nutritional Values: High Omega-3 (DHA, EPA) concentration, vitamin D.

- **Eggshell Powder**

Nutritional Values: Calcium.

- **Probiotics**

Nutritional Values: Support digestive health.

Amount of Ingredients per Dog Size

Dog Size	Sardines (cans)	Oats (cups, uncooked)	Carrots (cups, chopped)	Fish Oil (teaspoons)	Eggshell Powder (teaspoons)	Probiotics (capsules)
Small (up to 11 lbs.)	1/2 can	1/4 cup	1/4 cup	1/2 tsp	1/4 tsp	1/4 capsule
Medium (12-33 lbs.)	1 can	1/2 cup	1/2 cup	1 tsp	1/2 tsp	1/2 capsule
Large (34-66 lbs.)	1.5 cans	1 cup	1 cup	2 tsp	1 tsp	1 capsule
Very Large (67-99 lbs.)	2 cans	1.5 cups	1.5 cups	3 tsp	1.5 tsp	1.5 capsules
Giant (over 100 lbs.)	2.5 cans	2 cups	2 cups	4 tsp	2 tsp	2 capsules

Nutritional Values per Serving (for medium dog, 12-33 lbs.)

- **Calories**: ~300-350 kcal
- **Protein**: ~25-30 g
- **Fat**: ~10-15 g
- **Carbohydrates**: ~30-35 g
- **Fiber**: ~4-5 g
- **Vitamin A**: ~5000 IU
- **Omega-3**: ~600-700 mg

Preparation Times

- **Prep**: 15 minutes
- **Cook**: 10 minutes
- **Total**: 25 minutes

Procedure

1. Cook Oats

- Place oats in a pot with water (1:2 oats to water ratio).
- Bring to a boil, reduce heat, and simmer for 10 minutes or until tender.

2. Prepare Carrots

- In a pan, cook carrots with some water until tender (about 10 minutes).

3. Combine Ingredients

- Mix the canned sardines (drained), cooked oats, and cooked carrots in a large bowl.
- Add fish oil, eggshell powder, and probiotics.
- Toss well to ensure all ingredients are evenly distributed.

4. Let It Cool

- Let the food cool completely before serving.

Sardines and Brown Rice with Spinach

Ingredients

- **Sardines (canned in water, boneless, and skinless)**

Nutritional Values: High in Omega-3 fatty acids (DHA, EPA), protein, vitamins B12 and D, and calcium.

- **Brown Rice**

Nutritional Values: Complex carbohydrates, fiber, B vitamins (B1, B3, B6), magnesium, phosphorus.

- **Spinach**

Nutritional Values: Rich in vitamins A, C, K, folate, and iron.

- **Fish Oil**

Nutritional Values: High Omega-3 (DHA, EPA) concentration, vitamin D.

- **Eggshell Powder**

Nutritional Values: Calcium.

- **Probiotics**

Nutritional Values: Support digestive health.

Amount of Ingredients per Dog Size

Dog Size	Sardines (cans)	Brown Rice (cups, uncooked)	Spinach (cups, chopped)	Fish Oil (teaspoons)	Eggshell Powder (teaspoons)	Probiotics (capsules)
Small (up to 11 lbs.)	1/2 can	1/4 cup	1/4 cup	1/2 tsp	1/4 tsp	1/4 capsule
Medium (12-33 lbs.)	1 can	1/2 cup	1/2 cup	1 tsp	1/2 tsp	1/2 capsule
Large (34-66 lbs.)	1.5 cans	1 cup	1 cup	2 tsp	1 tsp	1 capsule
Very Large (67-99 lbs.)	2 cans	1.5 cups	1.5 cups	3 tsp	1.5 tsp	1.5 capsules
Giant (over 100 lbs.)	2.5 cans	2 cups	2 cups	4 tsp	2 tsp	2 capsules

Nutritional Values per Serving (for medium dog, 12-33 lbs)

- **Calories**: ~300-350 kcal
- **Protein**: ~25-30 g
- **Fat**: ~10-15 g
- **Carbohydrates**: ~30-35 g
- **Fiber**: ~4-5 g

- **Vitamin A**: ~5000 IU
- **Omega-3**: ~600-700 mg

Preparation Times

- **Prep**: 15 minutes
- **Cook**: 30 minutes
- **Total**: 45 minutes

Procedure

1. Cook Brown Rice

- Place rice in a pot with water (1:2 rice to water ratio).
- Bring to a boil, reduce heat, and cover.
- Cook for about 30 minutes or until rice is tender.

2. Prepare Spinach

- In a pan, cook Spinach with some water until it is wilted (about 3-5 minutes).

3. Combine Ingredients

- Mix the canned sardines (drained), cooked brown rice, and cooked Spinach in a large bowl.
- Add fish oil, eggshell powder, and probiotics.
- Toss well to ensure all ingredients are evenly distributed.

4. Let It Cool

- Let the food cool completely before serving.

Chapter 17

TROUT RECIPES

Trout and Quinoa with Zucchini

Ingredients

- **Trout (fresh or frozen, boneless and skinless)**

Nutritional Values: High in Omega-3 fatty acids (DHA, EPA), protein, vitamins B12 and D, selenium.

- **Quinoa**

Nutritional Values: Complete protein, high in fiber, B vitamins (B1, B2, B6), magnesium, phosphorus.

- **Zucchini**

Nutritional Values: Low in calories, high in vitamins A and C, potassium, fiber.

- **Fish Oil**

Nutritional Values: High concentration of Omega-3 (DHA, EPA), vitamin D.

- **Eggshell Powder**

Nutritional Values: Calcium.

- **Probiotics**

Nutritional Values: Support digestive health.

Amount of Ingredients per Dog Size

Dog Size	Trout (lbs)	Quinoa (cups, uncooked)	Zucchini (cups, chopped)	Fish Oil (teaspoons)	Eggshell Powder (teaspoons)	Probiotics (capsules)
Small (up to 11 lbs)	0.5 lbs	1/4 cup	1/4 cup	1/2 tsp	1/4 tsp	1/4 capsule
Medium (12-33 lbs)	1 lbs	1/2 cup	1/2 cup	1 tsp	1/2 tsp	1/2 capsule
Large (34-66 lbs)	1.5 lbs	1 cup	1 cup	2 tsp	1 tsp	1 capsule
Very Large (67-99 lbs)	2 lbs	1.5 cups	1.5 cups	3 tsp	1.5 tsp	1.5 capsules
Giant (over 100 lbs)	2.5 lbs	2 cups	2 cups	4 tsp	2 tsp	2 capsules

Nutritional Values per Serving (for medium dog, 12-33 lbs)

- **Calories:** ~350-400 kcal
- **Protein:** ~30-35 g
- **Fat:** ~15-20 g
- **Carbohydrates:** ~30-35 g
- **Fiber:** ~4-5 g
- **Vitamin A:** ~6000 IU
- **Omega-3:** ~700-800 mg

Preparation Times

- **Prep:** 15 minutes
- **Cook:** 25 minutes
- **Total:** 40 minutes

Procedure

1. Cook Quinoa

- Rinse quinoa under cold water.
- Place quinoa in a pot with water (1:2 quinoa to water ratio).
- Bring to a boil, reduce heat, cover, and simmer for about 15 minutes or until quinoa is tender.

2. Cook Trout

- In a pan, cook trout over medium heat until fully cooked (about 10 minutes).
- Flake the trout into bite-sized pieces and remove any bones.

3. Prepare Zucchini

- In a separate pan, cook zucchini with a little water until tender (about 5-7 minutes).

4. Combine Ingredients

- In a large bowl, mix the cooked trout, quinoa, and zucchini.
- Add fish oil, eggshell powder, and probiotics.
- Toss well to ensure all ingredients are evenly distributed.

5. Let It Cool

- Let the food cool completely before serving.

Trout and Sweet Potatoes with Broccoli

Ingredients

- **Trout (fresh or frozen, boneless and skinless)**

Nutritional Values: High in Omega-3 fatty acids (DHA, EPA), protein, vitamins B12 and D, selenium.

- **Sweet Potatoes**

Nutritional Values: High in beta-carotene (vitamin A), vitamin C, fiber, potassium.

- **Broccoli**

Nutritional Values: Rich in vitamins C, K, folate, fiber, and antioxidants.

- **Fish Oil**

Nutritional Values: High concentration of Omega-3 (DHA, EPA), vitamin D.

- **Eggshell Powder**

Nutritional Values: Calcium.

- **Probiotics**

Nutritional Values: Support digestive health.

Amount of Ingredients per Dog Size

Dog Size	Trout (lbs)	Sweet Potatoes (cups, chopped)	Broccoli (cups, chopped)	Fish Oil (teaspoons)	Eggshell Powder (teaspoons)	Probiotics (capsules)
Small (up to 11 lbs)	0.5 lbs	1/4 cup	1/4 cup	1/2 tsp	1/4 tsp	1/4 capsule
Medium (12-33 lbs)	1 lbs	1/2 cup	1/2 cup	1 tsp	1/2 tsp	1/2 capsule
Large (34-66 lbs)	1.5 lbs	1 cup	1 cup	2 tsp	1 tsp	1 capsule
Very Large (67-99 lbs)	2 lbs	1.5 cups	1.5 cups	3 tsp	1.5 tsp	1.5 capsules
Giant (over 100 lbs)	2.5 lbs	2 cups	2 cups	4 tsp	2 tsp	2 capsules

Nutritional Values per Serving (for medium dog, 12-33 lbs)

- **Calories:** ~350-400 kcal
- **Protein:** ~30-35 g
- **Fat:** ~15-20 g
- **Carbohydrates:** ~30-35 g
- **Fiber:** ~4-5 g

- **Vitamin A:** ~6000 IU
- **Omega-3:** ~700-800 mg

Preparation Times

- Prep: 15 minutes
- Cook: 30 minutes
- Total: 45 minutes

Procedure

1. Cook Sweet Potatoes

- Place sweet potatoes in a pot with water.
- Bring to a boil, reduce heat, and cook until tender (about 20 minutes).
- Drain and mash.

2. Cook Trout

- In a pan, cook trout over medium heat until fully cooked (about 10 minutes).
- Flake the trout into bite-sized pieces and remove any bones.

3. Prepare Broccoli

- In a separate pan, cook broccoli with a little water until tender (about 10 minutes).

4. Combine Ingredients

- In a large bowl, mix the cooked trout, mashed sweet potatoes, and cooked broccoli.
- Add fish oil, eggshell powder, and probiotics.
- Toss well to ensure all ingredients are evenly distributed.

5. Let It Cool

- Let the food cool completely before serving.

Chapter 18

EGG RECIPES

Eggs and Oats with Zucchini

Ingredients

- **Eggs**

Nutritional Values: High in protein, vitamins B2, B12, D, and minerals like selenium and zinc.

- **Oats**

Nutritional Values: Good source of fiber, B vitamins (B1, B5), magnesium, iron, and antioxidants.

- **Zucchini**

Nutritional Values: Low in calories, high in vitamins A and C, potassium, fiber.

- **Fish Oil**

Nutritional Values: High concentration of Omega-3 (DHA, EPA), vitamin D.

- **Eggshell Powder**

Nutritional Values: Calcium.

- **Probiotics**

Nutritional Values: Support digestive health.

Amount of Ingredients per Dog Size

Dog Size	Eggs (count)	Oats (cups,	Zucchini	Fish Oil	Eggshell Powder	Probiotics

		uncooked)	(cups, chopped)	(teaspoons)	(teaspoons)	(capsules)
Small (up to 11 lbs)	1 egg	1/4 cup	1/4 cup	1/2 tsp	1/4 tsp	1/4 capsule
Medium (12-33 lbs)	2 eggs	1/2 cup	1/2 cup	1 tsp	1/2 tsp	1/2 capsule
Large (34-66 lbs)	3 eggs	1 cup	1 cup	2 tsp	1 tsp	1 capsule
Very Large (67-99 lbs)	4 eggs	1.5 cups	1.5 cups	3 tsp	1.5 tsp	1.5 capsules
Giant (over 100 lbs)	5 eggs	2 cups	2 cups	4 tsp	2 tsp	2 capsules

Nutritional Values per Serving (for medium dog, 12-33 lbs)

- **Calories:** ~300-350 kcal
- **Protein:** ~20-25 g
- **Fat:** ~10-15 g
- **Carbohydrates:** ~25-30 g
- **Fiber:** ~3-4 g
- **Vitamin A:** ~3000 IU
- **Omega-3:** ~400-500 mg

Preparation Times

- Prep: 10 minutes
- Cook: 15 minutes
- Total: 25 minutes

Procedure

1. Cook Oats

- Place oats in a pot with water (1:2 oats to water ratio).
- Bring to a boil, reduce heat, and simmer until tender (about 10 minutes).

2. Cook Eggs

- In a pan, scramble or cook eggs until fully done (about 5 minutes).

3. Prepare Zucchini

- In a separate pan, cook zucchini with a little water until tender (about 5-7 minutes).

4. Combine Ingredients

- In a large bowl, mix cooked oats, scrambled eggs, and zucchini.
- Add fish oil, eggshell powder, and probiotics.
- Toss well to ensure all ingredients are evenly distributed.

5. Let It Cool

- Let the food cool completely before serving.

Eggs and Brown Rice with Pumpkin

Ingredients

- **Eggs**

Nutritional Values: High in protein, vitamins B2, B12, D, and minerals like selenium and zinc.

- **Brown Rice**

Nutritional Values: Complex carbohydrates, fiber, B vitamins (B1, B3, B6), magnesium, phosphorus.

- **Pumpkin**

Nutritional Values: High in beta-carotene (vitamin A), vitamin C, fiber, potassium.

- **Fish Oil**

Nutritional Values: High concentration of Omega-3 (DHA, EPA), vitamin D.

- **Eggshell Powder**

Nutritional Values: Calcium.

- **Probiotics**

Nutritional Values: Support digestive health.

Amount of Ingredients per Dog Size

Dog Size	Eggs (count)	Brown Rice (cups, uncooked)	Pumpkin (cups, chopped)	Fish Oil (teaspoons)	Eggshell Powder (teaspoons)	Probiotics (capsules)
Small (up to 11 lbs)	1 egg	1/4 cup	1/4 cup	1/2 tsp	1/4 tsp	1/4 capsule
Medium (12-33 lbs)	2 eggs	1/2 cup	1/2 cup	1 tsp	1/2 tsp	1/2 capsule
Large (34-66 lbs)	3 eggs	1 cup	1 cup	2 tsp	1 tsp	1 capsule
Very Large (67-99 lbs)	4 eggs	1.5 cups	1.5 cups	3 tsp	1.5 tsp	1.5 capsules
Giant (over 100 lbs)	5 eggs	2 cups	2 cups	4 tsp	2 tsp	2 capsules

Nutritional Values per Serving (for medium dog, 12-33 lbs)

- **Calories:** ~300-350 kcal
- **Protein:** ~20-25 g
- **Fat:** ~10-15 g
- **Carbohydrates:** ~30-35 g
- **Fiber:** ~4-5 g
- **Vitamin A:** ~5000 IU
- **Omega-3:** ~400-500 mg

Preparation Times

- Prep: 10 minutes
- Cook: 30 minutes
- Total: 40 minutes

Procedure

1. Cook Brown Rice

- Place rice in a pot with water (1:2 rice to water ratio).
- Bring to a boil, reduce heat, and cover.
- Cook for about 30 minutes or until rice is tender.

2. Cook Eggs

- In a pan, scramble or cook eggs until fully done (about 5 minutes).

3. Prepare Pumpkin

- In a separate pan, cook pumpkin with a little water until tender (about 10 minutes).

4. Combine Ingredients

- In a large bowl, mix cooked brown rice, eggs, and pumpkin.
- Add fish oil, eggshell powder, and probiotics.
- Toss well to ensure all ingredients are evenly distributed.

5. Let It Cool

- Let the food cool completely before serving.

Eggs and Sweet Potatoes with Carrots

Ingredients

- **Eggs**

Nutritional Values: High in protein, vitamins B2, B12, D, and minerals like selenium and zinc.

- **Sweet Potatoes**

Nutritional Values: High in beta-carotene (vitamin A), vitamin C, fiber, potassium.

- **Carrots**

Nutritional Values: Rich in beta-carotene (vitamin A), vitamin C, vitamin K, fiber.

- **Fish Oil**

Nutritional Values: High concentration of Omega-3 (DHA, EPA), vitamin D.

- **Eggshell Powder**

Nutritional Values: Calcium.

- **Probiotics**

Nutritional Values: Support digestive health.

Amount of Ingredients per Dog Size

Dog Size	Eggs (count)	Sweet Potatoes (cups, chopped)	Carrots (cups, chopped)	Fish Oil (teaspoons)	Eggshell Powder (teaspoons)	Probiotics (capsules)
Small (up to 11 lbs)	1 egg	1/4 cup	1/4 cup	1/2 tsp	1/4 tsp	1/4 capsule
Medium (12-33 lbs)	2 eggs	1/2 cup	1/2 cup	1 tsp	1/2 tsp	1/2 capsule
Large (34-66 lbs)	3 eggs	1 cup	1 cup	2 tsp	1 tsp	1 capsule
Very Large (67-99 lbs)	4 eggs	1.5 cups	1.5 cups	3 tsp	1.5 tsp	1.5 capsules
Giant (over 100 lbs)	5 eggs	2 cups	2 cups	4 tsp	2 tsp	2 capsules

Nutritional Values per Serving (for medium dog, 12-33 lbs)

- **Calories:** ~300-350 kcal
- **Protein:** ~20-25 g
- **Fat:** ~10-15 g
- **Carbohydrates:** ~30-35 g
- **Fiber:** ~4-5 g
- **Vitamin A:** ~5000 IU

- **Omega-3:** ~400-500 mg

Preparation Times

- Prep: 10 minutes
- Cook: 30 minutes
- Total: 40 minutes

Procedure

1. Cook Sweet Potatoes

- Place sweet potatoes in a pot with water.
- Bring to a boil, reduce heat, and cook until tender (about 20 minutes).
- Drain and mash.

2. Cook Eggs

- In a pan, scramble or cook eggs until fully done (about 5 minutes).
- Prepare Carrots
- In a separate pan, cook carrots with a little water until tender (about 10 minutes).

3. Combine Ingredients

- In a large bowl, mix cooked sweet potatoes, scrambled eggs, and carrots.
- Add fish oil, eggshell powder, and probiotics.
- Toss well to ensure all ingredients are evenly distributed.

5. Let It Cool

- Let the food cool completely before serving.

Chapter 19

PRESERVING OUR DOG'S EYES

The eyes are the most expressive part of a dog's body. They provide essential sensory information and impact the dog's quality of life. To understand the health of your dog's eyes, we have to look at different eye issues, how to address these problems, and how to implement preventive measures. This chapter will help you provide a detailed guide on how to preserve and maintain healthy eyes in dogs, including the anatomy of the eye, common eye conditions, treatment options, and preventive care.

UNDERSTANDING DOG EYE ANATOMY

Basic Anatomy of the Dog Eye

Cornea: It is the transparent front part of the eye. It covers the pupil and iris. It helps focus light onto the retina.

Iris: It is the colorful part of the eye. Its function is to control the size of the pupil and the amount of light that enters the eye.

Pupil: The black central part of the eye can be adjusted to let light in at the appropriate amount.

Lens: The lens is located behind the iris and focuses light onto the retina.

Retina: This is the light-sensitive layer at the back of the eye, and its role is to convert light into electrical signals that are sent to the brain.

Optic Nerve: The nerve transmits visual information from the retina to the brain.

Conjunctiva: The thin membrane covering the white part of the eye (sclera) and the inner surface of the eyelids.

Functions of the Eye

Vision: The primary function of the eye is to enable the dogs to see their environment.

Protection: The tear production and blink reflexes protect the eye from irritants and foreign bodies.

Communication: Dog express many of their emotions and intentions through eye contact and movement.

COMMON EYE CONDITIONS IN DOGS

Conjunctivitis:

It is referred to as "pink eye." In this eye condition, the inflammation of the conjunctiva occurs.

Symptoms: Redness, discharge, swelling, and itching.

Causes: Allergies, infections, irritants, or foreign bodies.

Treatment: Depending on the cause, treatment may include antibiotics, anti-inflammatory medications, or antihistamines.

Cataracts:

In this eye condition, lens clouding leads to blindness and vision impairment.

Symptoms: Eye appearance becomes cloudy, vision difficulty, and potentially behavioral changes occur.

Causes: Genetics, diabetes, trauma, or aging.

Treatment: Surgical removal of the cataract is often recommended.

Glaucoma

In this condition, increased intraocular pressure usually leads to potential blindness and pain.

Symptoms: Redness, bulging of the eye, squinting, and behavioral changes such as reluctance to move.

Causes: Genetic predisposition secondary to other eye conditions.

Treatment: For this eye condition, medications can be used to reduce pressure, and sometimes, surgical interventions are necessary.

Dry Eye (Keratoconjunctivitis Sicca)

In this condition, insufficient teat production leads to inflamed and dry eyes.

Symptoms: Redness, discharge, squinting, and a dry appearance.

Causes: Autoimmune conditions, certain medications, or genetic factors.

Treatment: Dogs can be given certain medications to stimulate tear production or manage the underlying cause.

Cherry Eye

A prolapse in the third eye gland results in a red swollen mass in the corner of the eye.

Symptoms: Visible red mass, discomfort, and possible discharge.

Causes: Genetic factors or weak connective tissues.

Treatment: Usually, the gland is removed or repositioned through surgery

Uveitis

In this condition, inflammation of the uvea (the middle layer of the eye) occurs.

Symptoms: Redness, pain, squinting, and sensitivity to light.

Causes: Infection, trauma, or systemic diseases.

Treatment: In this condition, anti-inflammatory medication is given, sometimes addressing the underlying cause.

Eye Injuries

Trauma to the eye or surrounding tissues.

Symptoms: Redness, swelling, tearing, or visible injury.

Causes: Scratches, foreign bodies, or blunt trauma.

Treatment: Urgent veterinary care is given to prevent complications and provide appropriate treatment.

PREVENTIVE CARE FOR DOG EYES

Regular Eye Examinations

Frequency: Visit your veterinary specialist annually so that early signs of the eye can be detected, and we will be able to maintain the overall eye health.

Components: A vet expert examines the animal for signs of infection, irritation, and general health.

Proper Grooming

Cleaning: Don't use harsh chemicals. To maintain cleanliness, softly clean the area around the eye with a damp, soft cloth to remove any debris or discharge.

Hair Trimming: If the dog belongs to a breed that has fur around its eyes, trim that hair to avoid obstructive vision and irritation.

Eye Protection

Outdoor Activities: Protect your dog's eyes from wind, sunlight, and debris during outdoor activities. If needed, use dog-specific goggles.

Preventing Injury: Supervise your dog during playtime so that you can avoid any potential injuries from rough play and environmental hazards.

Nutrition and Supplements

Balanced Diet: Provide a completely balanced diet that supports the overall well-being of the dog, including eye health. Omega-3 fatty acids and antioxidants like vitamin E contribute to maintaining healthy eyes.

Supplements: Book a consultation with your veterinarian for suggestions about supplements that might support eye health, particularly for breeds predisposed to eye conditions.

RECOGNIZING SIGNS OF EYE PROBLEMS

Behavioral Changes

Signs: If your dog is rubbing his eyes or showing resistance to participating in or enjoying the activities he used to play earlier, this could be an indicator that there is some eye issue.

Action: Observe these behaviors closely and consult your veterinarian if symptoms persist.

Physical Symptoms

Signs: Look for redness, swelling, excessive tearing, discharge, or changes in the appearance of the eyes.

Action: Contact your veterinarian to evaluate the cause and appropriate treatment.

TREATMENT AND MANAGEMENT

Veterinary Care

Initial Examination: A complete eye examination from a veterinarian is necessary to diagnose and treat the eye condition.

Specialist Referral: In case of complex or severe eye conditions, referral to a veterinary ophthalmologist may be necessary.

Medications

Eye Drops/Ointments: Follow your veterinarian's instructions for applying medications. Use only products prescribed for your dog to avoid further irritation.

Oral Medications: In some cases, systemic medications may be required to treat underlying conditions affecting the eyes.

Surgery

Indications: Surgical interventions for conditions like cherry eye or cataracts might be necessary.

Recovery: Follow post-surgical care instructions for proper healing and to avoid complications.

EMERGENCY SITUATIONS

Immediate Response

Trauma: If your dog experiences trauma or an eye injury, seek veterinary care immediately to prevent any serious damage.

Foreign Objects: If a foreign object is lodged in the eye, avoid attempting to remove it yourself and consult a veterinarian.

Recognizing Urgency

Symptoms: If there is any severe pain, noticeable vision loss, or significant discharge, urgently seek veterinary attention.

PREVENTION OF EYE DISEASES

Maintaining optimal eye health in dogs includes a proactive approach to averting eye diseases. Common eye conditions in dogs include conjunctivitis, cataracts, glaucoma, and cataracts. To prevent these issues:

Regular Check-ups: Plan annual vet visits to monitor eye health and catch early signs of problems.

Proper Nutrition: Try to provide your dog with a balanced diet that is rich in antioxidants, omega fatty acids, and vitamins that support eye health.

Protect from Irritants: Minimize exposure to dust, smoke, and chemicals that can damage your dog's eye.

Hygiene: Keep your eyes clean and free from dust. Regularly wipe away discharge with a damp cloth.

BETTER QUALITY OF LIFE

Healthy eyes play a significant role in a dog's quality of life. Having a clear vision allows dogs to:

Navigate Effectively: Dogs rely on visualization to steer their environment safely. Maintaining good eye health helps them avoid obstacles and reduce the risk of accidents.

Engage in Activities: Clear vision boosts their capability to play and engage in activities they enjoy, such as fetch or new environments.

DETECTION OF HEALTH PROBLEMS

Poor eye conditions can sometimes lead to broader health issues. For example:

Diabetes: Diabetic dogs may develop cataracts. Regular eye exams can help detect such conditions early.

Thyroid Issues: Hypothyroidism can lead to changes in the eyes. Monitoring eye health can provide clues about underlying thyroid problems.

NAVIGATION AND SAFETY

Proper vision is essential for a dog's navigation and safety:

Avoiding Hazards: Dogs with good visualization can better avoid hazards like sharp objects, stairs, or traffic.

Practical Training: Dogs need visual cues for training commands and interactions. Good eyesight supports actual communication and training.

Below are recipes that have ingredients especially beneficial for a dog's eye sight, containing essential nutrients and supplements.

Salmon and Sweet Potatoes with Spinach and Blueberries

Ingredients

- **Salmon**

Nutritional Values: High in Omega-3 fatty acids (DHA, EPA), protein, vitamins B12 and D, and selenium.

- **Sweet Potatoes**

Nutritional Values: High in beta-carotene (vitamin A), vitamin C, fiber, and potassium.

- **Spinach**

Nutritional Values: Rich in vitamins A, C, and K, iron, calcium, and antioxidants.

- **Blueberries**

Nutritional Values: High in antioxidants, vitamin C, vitamin K, and fiber.

- **Fish Oil**

Nutritional Values: High Omega-3 (DHA, EPA) concentration, vitamin D.

- **Eggshell Powder**

Nutritional Values: Calcium.

- **Probiotics**

Nutritional Values: Support digestive health.

Amount of Ingredients per Dog Size

Dog Size	Salmon (lbs.)	Sweet Potatoes (cups, chopped)	Spinach (cups, chopped)	Blueberries (cups)	Fish Oil (teaspoons)	Eggshell Powder (teaspoons)
Small (up to 11 lbs.)	0.5 lbs.	1/4 cup	1/4 cup	1/4 cup	1/2 tsp	1/4 tsp
Medium (12-33 lbs)	1 lbs	1/2 cup	1/2 cup	1/2 cup	1 tsp	1/2 tsp
Large (34-66 lbs)	1.5 lbs	1 cup	1 cup	1 cup	2 tsp	1 tsp
Very Large (67-99 lbs)	2 lbs	1.5 cups	1.5 cups	1.5 cups	3 tsp	1.5 tsp

Giant (over 100 lbs)	2.5 lbs	2 cups	2 cups	2 cups	4 tsp	2 tsp

Nutritional Values per Serving (for medium dog, 12-33 lbs)

- **Calories:** ~350-400 kcal
- **Protein:** ~25-30 g
- **Fat:** ~15-20 g
- **Carbohydrates:** ~30-35 g
- **Fiber:** ~5-6 g
- **Vitamin A:** ~6000 IU
- **Omega-3:** ~600-700 mg

Preparation Times

- Prep: 15 minutes
- Cook: 30 minutes
- Total: 45 minutes

Procedure

1. Cook Sweet Potatoes

- Place sweet potatoes in a pot with water.
- Bring to a boil, reduce heat, and cook until tender (about 20 minutes).
- Drain and mash.

2. Cook Salmon

- Place salmon in a pan with a bit of water or oil.
- Cook over medium heat for 10-15 minutes or until fully cooked.
- Flake the salmon into bite-sized pieces.

3. Prepare Spinach

- In a pan, cook spinach with water until wilted (about 5 minutes).

4. Combine Ingredients

- Mix cooked salmon, sweet potatoes, spinach, and blueberries in a large bowl.
- Add fish oil, eggshell powder, and probiotics.
- Toss well to ensure all ingredients are evenly distributed.

5. Let It Cool

- Let the food cool completely before serving.

Turkey and Pumpkin with Broccoli and Blueberries

Ingredients

- **Turkey**

Nutritional Values: Rich in lean protein, vitamins B6 and B12, niacin, and selenium.

- **Pumpkin**

Nutritional Values: High in beta-carotene (vitamin A), vitamin C, fiber, and potassium.

- **Broccoli**

Nutritional Values: High in vitamins C and K, fiber, antioxidants, and calcium.

- **Blueberries**

Nutritional Values: High in antioxidants, vitamin C, vitamin K, and fiber.

- **Fish Oil**

Nutritional Values: High Omega-3 (DHA, EPA) concentration, vitamin D.

- **Eggshell Powder**

Nutritional Values: Calcium.

- **Probiotics**

Nutritional Values: Support digestive health.

Amount of Ingredients per Dog Size

Dog Size	Turkey (lbs)	Pumpkin (cups, chopped)	Broccoli (cups, chopped)	Blueberries (cups)	Fish Oil (teaspoons)	Eggshell Powder (teaspoons)
Small (up to 11 lbs)	0.5 lbs	1/4 cup	1/4 cup	1/4 cup	1/2 tsp	1/4 tsp
Medium (12-33 lbs)	1 lbs	1/2 cup	1/2 cup	1/2 cup	1 tsp	1/2 tsp
Large (34-66 lbs)	1.5 lbs	1 cup	1 cup	1 cup	2 tsp	1 tsp
Very Large	2 lbs	1.5 cups	1.5 cups	1.5 cups	3 tsp	1.5 tsp

(67-99 lbs)						
Giant (over 100 lbs)	2.5 lbs	2 cups	2 cups	2 cups	4 tsp	2 tsp

Nutritional Values per Serving (for medium dog, 12-33 lbs)

- **Calories:** ~350-400 kcal
- **Protein:** ~25-30 g
- **Fat:** ~15-20 g
- **Carbohydrates:** ~30-35 g
- **Fiber:** ~5-6 g
- **Vitamin A:** ~6000 IU
- **Omega-3:** ~600-700 mg

Preparation Times

- Prep: 15 minutes
- Cook: 30 minutes
- Total: 45 minutes

Procedure

1. Cook Pumpkin

- Place pumpkin in a pot with water.
- Bring to a boil, reduce heat, and cook until tender (about 15-20 minutes).
- Drain and mash.

2. Cook Turkey

- Place turkey in a pan with a bit of water or oil.
- Cook over medium heat for 15-20 minutes or until fully cooked.
- Cut the turkey into bite-sized pieces.

3. Prepare Broccoli

- In a separate pan, steam or cook Broccoli until tender (about 10 minutes).

4. Combine Ingredients

- Mix cooked turkey, pumpkin, Broccoli, and blueberries in a large bowl.
- Add fish oil, eggshell powder, and probiotics.
- Toss well to ensure all ingredients are evenly distributed.

5. Let It Cool

- Let the food cool completely before serving.

Chapter 20

PRESERVING OUR DOG'S SKIN

The skin of dogs does more than you think. Healthy skin can be identified by its shiny coat. It helps to prevent infections and plays an important role in dogs' comfort. This chapter will help you explore the various aspects of maintaining and preserving your dog's skin health, like the role of nutrition in improving your dog's skin, environmental factors, grooming practices, common skin issues, and preventive measures.

UNDERSTANDING DOG SKIN STRUCTURE

Skin Layers and Functions

Epidermis: This is the outmost layer of dog skin that provides a protective barrier against environmental hazards and pathogens. It contains keratinocytes that produce keratin, a protein that strengthens the skin.

Dermis: This is the middle layer that contains hair follicles, blood vessels, sweat glands, and connective tissues. It houses nerves that detect temperature and pain and provides structural support.

Hypodermis: This is the deepest layer, composed of connective tissues and fats. It acts as a shock absorber and insulator.

Skin Functions

Protection: The skin acts as a protector to protect internal organs and systems from environmental pathogens and damage.

Temperature Regulation: Sweating and panting help maintain average body temperature.

Sensory Perception: It is based on the sensory receptors that detect pain, touch, and body temperature.

Essential Nutrients

- ***Fatty Acids:*** Omega-6 and Omega-3 fatty acids are important for maintaining skin moisture and lessening inflammation. You can get these fatty acids from flaxseed oil, fish oil, and certain animal fats.
- ***Proteins:*** A sufficient protein intake also supports regeneration and skin repair. The best sources of protein are beef, chicken, and fish.

Vitamins:

- ***Vitamin A:*** It helps in skin cell production and repair. It is found in carrots, livers, and sweet potatoes.
- ***Vitamin E*** is an antioxidant that protects the skin from oxidative damage. It is found in leafy greens and vegetable oils.
- ***Vitamin C***: It helps produce collagen, which is essential for skin elasticity. It is found in fruits like vegetables like bell peppers and fruits like oranges.

Hydration

Water: Make sure your dog is drinking clean and fresh water. This is important for maintaining skin hydration and overall health, as adequate hydration prevents dryness and supports skin elasticity.

GROOMING PRACTICES

Brushing

Frequency: Regular brushing helps to remove dirt, debris, and fur and reduces the risk of skin matting and infection. How frequently your dog needs to be brushed depends on its coat type.

Tools: Use brushes accordingly for different coat types. For long coats, you can use slicker brushes, while for short coats, use bristle brushes.

Bathing

Frequency: The Dog's coat type, skin condition, and activity level will help you identify how frequently bathing should be done. Excessive bathing can strip the skin of natural oils.

Shampoo: Try to use a dog-specific shampoo that is free of harsh chemicals. If your dog has sensitive skin or any skin issues, then use medicated or hypoallergenic shampoos.

Conditioner: If your dog has a long, curly coat, use a conditioner to help detangle it and maintain coat moisture.

Nail Trimming

Importance: Trimming your nails on a regular basis helps you avoid any discomfort and potential skin issues that can cause nails to grow into the pads or cause an abnormal gait.

Technique: Try trimming your dogs' nails, and if you are unsure consult a veterinarian or groomer for guidance on proper nail care.

Ear Cleaning

Frequency: Regularly check ears for any signs of infection or a pile of wax. Clean it only when needed it.

Products: Consult a veterinary specialist for recommendations about ear cleaners to avoid irritation and ensure the product is suitable for your dog's ears.

ENVIRONMENTAL FACTORS

Allergens

Common Allergens: Dust mites, pollen, mold, and certain food ingredients can cause skin allergies. Observe for signs of allergic reaction like redness or itching.

Management: Avoid exposure to known allergens and only consider hypoallergenic dog food for environmental controls.

Temperature and Humidity

Weather Conditions: Extreme temperatures can affect your dog's skin health. Make sure your dog has appropriate shelter to be safe from different weather conditions and can maintain a comfortable indoor environment.

Humidity: Dry indoor air can also contribute to skin dryness. To maintain a moisture level, try using a humidifier.

Parasites

Fleas and Ticks: These parasites can cause various skin problems, such as irritation, itching, or skin infections. Use flea and tick prevention products recommended by your veterinarian.

Prevention: Check your dog regularly for signs of parasites and book a consultation with your vet to learn about the best preventive measures.

COMMON SKIN ISSUES

Allergies

Symptoms: swelling, redness, itching, and ear infection. Allergies can be food-related and environmental.

Treatment: Identify and avoid allergens, and use antihistamines or corticosteroids depending on what your veterinarian prescribes.

Hot Spots

Acute, moist dermatitis caused by excessive licking or scratching. Characterized by red, inflamed areas.

Treatment: Clean the area, apply topical antibiotics or anti-inflammatory medications, and prevent further licking.

Dry Skin

Symptoms: Flaky, itchy skin with possible hair loss. It can be caused by environmental factors or poor nutrition.

Treatment: Increase omega fatty acid intake, ensure proper hydration, and use moisturizing shampoos or conditioners.

Mange

It's a skin condition caused by mites. The symptoms include hair loss, skin infections, and severe itching.

Treatment: It requires veterinary diagnosis and treatment that usually involves systematic medications or medicated baths.

Ringworm

It is a fungal infection that leads to circular patches of skin irritation or hair loss.

Treatment: In this case, topical treatment and antifungal medications are prescribed by a veterinarian.

PREVENTATIVE MEASURES

Regular Veterinary Check-Ups

Importance: Regular vet visits are very important as they help detect early signs of skin issues and maintain overall skin health.

Examinations: Regular preventive screening and skin exams can easily catch the problem before it becomes severe.

Balanced Diet

Quality Food: Feed a high-quality, nutritionally balanced diet for skin health and coat condition.

Supplements: Consider adding skin and coat supplements if recommended by your veterinarian.

Hygiene and Cleanliness

Bedding: Keep your dog's bedding clean and free of parasites. Wash bedding regularly and ensure a clean sleeping environment.

Living Area: Maintain a clean living area to reduce exposure to allergens and contaminants.

Avoiding Harmful Products

Toxic Substances: Avoid using products with harsh chemicals or fragrances that can irritate your dog's skin.

Safety: Always choose pet-safe products and consult your veterinarian before introducing new grooming or health products.

Salmon and Sweet Potatoes with Spinach and Flaxseed

Ingredients

- **Salmon**

Nutritional Values: High protein, Omega-3 fatty acids (DHA, EPA), vitamins B12 and D, and selenium.

- **Sweet Potatoes**

Nutritional Values: High in beta-carotene (vitamin A), vitamin C, fiber, and potassium.

- **Spinach**

Nutritional Values: Rich in vitamins A, C, K, folate, iron, and calcium.

- **Flaxseed**

Nutritional Values: High in Omega-3 fatty acids (ALA), fiber, and lignans.

- **Fish Oil**

Nutritional Values: High Omega-3 (DHA, EPA) concentration, vitamin D.

- **Eggshell Powder**

Nutritional Values: Calcium.

- **Probiotics**

Nutritional Values: Support digestive health.

Amount of Ingredients per Dog Size

Dog Size	Salmon (cups, cooked)	Sweet Potatoes (cups, chopped)	Spinach (cups, chopped)	Flaxseed (teaspoons)	Fish Oil (teaspoons)	Eggshell Powder (teaspoons)
Small (up to 11 lbs)	1/2 cup	1/4 cup	1/4 cup	1/2 tsp	1/2 tsp	1/4 tsp
Medium (12-33 lbs)	1 cup	1/2 cup	1/2 cup	1 tsp	1 tsp	1/2 tsp
Large (34-66 lbs)	1.5 cups	1 cup	1 cup	1.5 tsp	2 tsp	1 tsp
Very Large (67-99 lbs)	2 cups	1.5 cups	1.5 cups	2 tsp	3 tsp	1.5 tsp
Giant (over 100 lbs)	3 cups	2 cups	2 cups	3 tsp	4 tsp	2 tsp

Nutritional Values per Serving (for medium dog, 12-33 lbs.)

- **Calories:** ~350-400 kcal
- **Protein:** ~25-30 g
- **Fat:** ~15-20 g
- **Carbohydrates:** ~30-35 g
- **Fiber:** ~5-6 g
- **Vitamin A:** ~5000 IU
- **Omega-3:** ~600-700 mg

Preparation Times

- Prep: 15 minutes
- Cook: 25 minutes
- Total: 40 minutes

Procedure

1. Cook Salmon

- Bake or grill salmon until fully cooked (about 15-20 minutes).

- Flake into small pieces and let cool.

2. Cook Sweet Potatoes

- Place sweet potatoes in a pot with water.
- Bring to a boil, reduce heat, and cook until tender (about 20 minutes).
- Drain and mash.

3. Prepare Spinach

- In a pan, cook spinach with a little water until wilted (about 5 minutes).

4. Combine Ingredients

- In a large bowl, mix cooked salmon, sweet potatoes, and spinach.
- Add flaxseed, fish oil, eggshell powder, and probiotics.
- Toss well to ensure all ingredients are evenly distributed.

5. Let It Cool

- Let the food cool completely before serving.

Turkey and Pumpkin with Coconut Oil and Carrots

Ingredients

- **Turkey**

Nutritional Values: High protein, vitamins B6 and B12, niacin, selenium, and zinc.

- **Pumpkin**

Nutritional Values: High in beta-carotene (vitamin A), vitamin C, fiber, and potassium.

- **Carrots**

Nutritional Values: Rich in beta-carotene (vitamin A), vitamin C, vitamin K, and fiber.

- **Coconut Oil**

Nutritional Values: Contains medium-chain triglycerides (MCTs), which may provide quick energy and support healthy skin and coat.

- **Fish Oil**

Nutritional Values: High Omega-3 (DHA, EPA) concentration, vitamin D.

- **Eggshell Powder**

Nutritional Values: Calcium.

- **Probiotics**

Nutritional Values: Support digestive health.

Amount of Ingredients per Dog Size

Dog Size	Pumpkin (cups, cooked)	Carrots (cups, chopped)	Coconut Oil (teaspoons)	Fish Oil (teaspoons)	Eggshell Powder (teaspoons)	Probiotics (capsules)
Small (up to 11 lbs)	1/4 cup	1/4 cup	1/2 tsp	1/2 tsp	1/4 tsp	1/4 capsule
Medium (12-33 lbs)	1/2 cup	1/2 cup	1 tsp	1 tsp	1/2 tsp	1/2 capsule
Large (34-66 lbs)	1 cup	1 cup	1.5 tsp	2 tsp	1 tsp	1 capsule
Very Large (67-99 lbs)	1.5 cups	1.5 cups	2 tsp	3 tsp	1.5 tsp	1.5 capsules
Giant (over 100 lbs)	2 cups	2 cups	3 tsp	4 tsp	2 tsp	2 capsules

Nutritional Values per Serving (for medium dog, 12-33 lbs.)

- **Calories:** ~350-400 kcal
- **Protein:** ~25-30 g
- **Fat:** ~15-20 g
- **Carbohydrates:** ~30-35 g

- **Fiber:** ~5-6 g
- **Vitamin A:** ~6000 IU
- **Omega-3:** ~400-500 mg

Preparation Times

- Prep: 15 minutes
- Cook: 30 minutes
- Total: 45 minutes

Procedure

1. Cook Turkey

- Cook ground turkey in a pan until entirely done (about 10 minutes).
- Drain any excess fat.

2. Cook Pumpkin

- Place pumpkin in a pot with water.
- Bring to a boil, reduce heat, and cook until tender (about 20 minutes).
- Drain and mash.

3. Prepare Carrots

- In a separate pan, cook carrots with water until tender (about 10 minutes).

4. Combine Ingredients

- In a large bowl, mix cooked turkey, pumpkin, and carrots.
- Add coconut oil, fish oil, eggshell powder, and probiotics.
- Toss well to ensure all ingredients are evenly distributed.

5. Let It Cool

- Let the food cool completely before serving.

CONCLUSION

During our reading, we've gone over several benefits of DIY dog food, including:

- ✓ **Customization:** Modify recipes to meet your dog's specific dietary needs and preferences.
- ✓ **Quality Control:** Use fresh, high-quality elements without unnecessary additives or preservatives.
- ✓ **Cost Efficiency:** Homemade meals can be more cost-effective than commercial options.
- ✓ **Health Benefits:** Homemade food can improve overall health, including better digestion, energy levels, and coat condition.

Boarding on the DIY dog food journey requires some effort and assurance, but the rewards are worth it. Providing your dog with new, nutritious meals can enhance their well-being, permanence, and happiness. Stay informed about their dietary needs, and don't hesitate to consult with your veterinarian for guidance and support.

We encourage you to share your experiences with DIY dog food. Whether it's a new recipe you've tried, adjustments you've made for your dog's needs, or simply your success stories, your intuitions can be invaluable to other dog owners. Sharing experiences not only nurtures a sense of community but also helps others offer the best care for their furry companions.

Let's work together to ensure every dog enjoys a healthier, happier life with the power of homemade nutrition.

Bonus

Thank you for reading my book "Dog Food Cookbook". I hope you found the information and recipes useful for your four-legged friends. Your dog's health and well-being are my top priorities and for this reason I want to offer you two exclusive bonuses that will help you get the most for your dog.

Snacks Bonus

Discover the world of dog snacks with our exclusive bonus! **Snacks** are not just a tasty reward but also an opportunity to supplement your furry friend's diet with essential nutrients. In this bonus, you will find easy and quick recipes to create healthy and delicious treats right in your kitchen. From crunchy biscuits to soft bites, each recipe is designed to satisfy your dog's palate and provide targeted nutritional benefits. Offer your loyal companion snacks made with love, free from additives and artificial preservatives, for a moment of joy and wellness!

Weekly Meal Planner

Optimize your dog's nutrition with our **Weekly Meal Planner**! This practical and easy-to-use tool will help you plan a week of balanced and varied meals for your four-legged friend. Additionally, there is space to note dietary preferences, special needs, and dietary variations. Save time in the kitchen and ensure your dog gets everything they need to stay healthy and happy. Meal planning has never been this simple!

Thank you for choosing The Ultimate dog Cookbook. Your dedication and love for your dog is truly inspiring and I am honored to be able to help you care for your friend.

Before you access the bonus content, I would really appreciate it if you could take a moment to leave a review on Amazon.

Your feedback helps me create new quality content.

You can simply scan the QR code to leave your review.

To receive these bonuses, you can scan the qr code below

I look forward to hearing from you and hearing how your dog feels after eating your succulent dishes.

With gratitude,

Petra Rice

Made in United States
Orlando, FL
01 June 2025